Wildlife throu_g

Encounters with birds, animals and plants

Tim Sharrock

with a Foreword by Bill Oddie

Published by J. T. R. Sharrock
Fountains, Park Lane, Blunham, Bedford MK44 3NJ

First published during 2002-2013 in the *Bedfordshire County Life Magazine*

ISBN 978-1-291-66252-8

Contents

Foreword *by Bill Oddie*

I live in London but am fortunate enough to be within walking distance of Hampstead Heath. This wondrously huge green space is many things to many people, but the one thing it is not is a heath. Well, there are a couple of tiny patches of gorse and heather, but they were planted by the London Wildlife Trust. However there are areas of ancient woodland, a few hedgerows, quite a lot of natural grassland and half a dozen small lakes. All in all a pretty good place to go searching for wildlife, which is what I do. I am not the lone birdwatcher, but we are totally outnumbered by literally hundreds of pram-pushers, kite-flyers, footballers, joggers, dog-walkers and of course dogs. A very high percentage of them are wearing earphones or dialling their mobiles, or both. (Not of course the dogs. Yet.)

I often wonder how many of these people hear birdsong or notice the wildflower patches (another Trust enterprise), or the Redwings in the hedgerows in autumn, or the Swallows migrating over their heads. One year, on the morning of 28th September, I estimated that at least 10,000 Swallows had flown over my part of London. Only two people asked me what I was looking at with my binoculars. They hadn't noticed the birds! Every now and then, I am approached by someone asking if they could have seen a parakeet. How could they not have?! Especially when there is a screeching flock of them. (Try removing the headphones. OK, it is not a pretty sound. Put them back on!) I was once asked "What are the big black birds perched on one of the pond's rafts?" "Cormorants," I replied. "Well, well. I have never seen them before," was the response, which surprised me, because I knew that this man had been walking past the ponds for as many years as the Cormorants had been perching on the rafts.

Watching wildlife is of course about looking and listening, but it is mainly about being aware. It helps to have a guide or a companion, an expert and a storyteller. Tim Sharrock is perfect for the job. Read this book, and then go and see for yourself. Oh, and by all means take the dog, but forget the earphones.

Bill Oddie
January 2014

Introduction

The observation of birds, mammals, butterflies and other insects and invertebrates, plants and fungi − natural history, in other words − is **fun**. We may do it casually, as a mere by-product of a country stroll, or more seriously or perhaps professionally, but even the most dedicated scientist **enjoys** it.

This book aims to demonstrate the wide range of natural sights and sounds that can excite anyone with an inquisitive outlook to life. It is divided into 'bite-sized' snippets or chapters that first appeared as articles in the quarterly *Bedfordshire County Life Magazine*. Enough bedtime reading for a whole year!

As well as the fifty sometimes serious, sometimes light-hearted, sometimes humorous articles, this book also contains an equal number of wildlife-based puzzles or quiz questions, intended to entertain (or sometimes to tease or infuriate) the reader. These are scattered through the book (the first one appears below, on this page), but the answers are all given on pages 155-159. There are 52 of them, so solve one a week if you can.

Now, have **fun**!

Wildlife Puzzle 1

Q. Why should a valuable molluscan product and the North American name for the Common Seal bring to mind an infamous 7th December?

Expect the unexpected!

My hosts had given me a suggested time of arrival, but had warned me that they might be a little late themselves. I was early, the house was deserted, and I had binoculars, *Barbour* jacket and Wellington boots in the car, so I opted to take a look at a nearby piece of rough ground instead of waiting impatiently in my car for my hosts to get back from work. What a good decision!

As I strolled along the footpath, a three-quarters moon was visible in the still-blue sky, and a couple of Redshanks chided each other in the distance, calling "chirrabim". A sight, a smell or a sound can be so evocative of a past experience, and in this case the Redshanks' cries brought back to me memories of the first time that I ever saw and heard 'The Watchdogs of the Marshes' (as they were formerly nicknamed), on the North Kent Marshes back in my schooldays.

Just enjoying the atmosphere, I raised my binoculars to look at a low-flying shape and, to my astonishment, saw that it was a hunting Short-eared Owl, working its way on silent wings along a grassy bank. After a few minutes, it drifted over the top of the bank and out of sight. Almost at once, however, a noisy gang of Jackdaws bickered in the distance, the reason soon becoming clear as they harassed a passing Sparrowhawk, once such a rare sight in eastern England, but now, happily, back to more-normal numbers after the end of the Pesticide Era of the third quarter of the twentieth century.

Reaching a gate across the path, I stopped to rest and contemplate the evening scene. Barely 20 metres away, the Sparrowhawk sat perched on the top of a fence-post: a juvenile, with streaked throat, thinly barred belly and broadly barred tail, its large size proclaiming that it was a young female (a large female can weigh three times as much as, and be 40% larger than, a small male). She was facing away from me, but two white spots on the back of her head looked like two eyes, and were quite enough to deter an even-larger predator. Whether because she sensed my presence or by pure chance, she suddenly turned, took off and swished past my head so close that I felt the whoosh of her wings. Was it chance that she passed so close? Or did my head briefly look like another and better lookout perch? Or did my pink and 'furry' face look like a tempting meal? I'll never know.

As I gathered my wits from this close encounter, a movement in the field beyond the gate revealed itself as a brown and mammalian rear end, but of what? The beast was facing directly away from me and had its head buried in the long grass, and neither shape nor colour 'rang any bells.' When it withdrew its head, however, and trotted across the field, it revealed itself as a Red Fox, its front half far more rufous than its dark greyish-brown rear quarters. It was doubtless out hunting mice and voles in the rough pastureland. The scene, with the rising moon now big and bright and orange, was like a painting.

A good time to go, so I turned to retrace my steps, and there, like a ghostly mobile, was a hunting Barn Owl, quartering the field across which I had just walked.

How glad I was that my hosts' absence had given me a totally unexpected, memorable, 30 minutes. That's what's so marvellous about almost any stroll in the country.

First published in *Bedfordshire County Life Magazine* in winter 2001/02

Spring has sprung

Spring has sprung
The grass has ris
I wonder where de boidies is?
[Anon.]

Every year, concerns are expressed about the decline of this, that or the other bird. "Nightingales are fewer, Sky Larks are doomed, and Song Thrushes have vanished." Yes, 'tis so, at least to some extent, but (and it is a big BUT) other species have increased, and good news seems to be no news in today's media.

In Bedfordshire today, Green Woodpeckers, Great Spotted Woodpeckers, Nuthatches, Grey Wagtails and a dozen other delightful species are far more numerous and widespread than they were twenty or thirty years ago, but have you heard any cheers of delight? Almost certainly not. You will probably, however, have heard about the increased numbers of "thieving Magpies", "killer Sparrowhawks" and "egg-stealing Carrion Crows." The media (including the natural history media) somehow manage to turn even good news into bad news.

The fact is that bird numbers, like all animal and plant populations, fluctuate in response to a huge range of external factors. At any one time, many species will be increasing in numbers and expanding their ranges (and extending into new habitats), whereas others will be declining in numbers, contracting their ranges and becoming extinct in marginal habitats. Some will be doing this on a relatively short-term cycle, others over a much longer time span. Superimposed on this will be interactions between them, changes in response to weather (hard winters or wet summers, for example), changes in response to climate (such as global warming) and changes in response to the effects of human activities (the creation of commercial forests or reservoirs, as well as the much publicised destruction of rainforests and marshland).

Here in Bedfordshire, Wrynecks, Red-backed Shrikes and Stone-curlews used to nest, but are now long gone. On the other hand, we have gained Collared Dove, Little Ringed Plover and Oystercatcher. [Even more recently, we have lost Woodcocks, Nightjars and Willow Tits, but have gained Red Kite, Common Buzzard, Peregrine and Raven.] Swings and roundabouts.

The conservation bodies are quite right to be concerned about the effects of agricultural intensification, the loss of wildlife habitat to building and road construction, and all the various forms of pollution. This spring, however, do please enjoy the birds and other wildlife that we do have. In mid March, the first Wheatears and Sand Martins will already have arrived back from Africa, and Swallows, Cuckoos and Swifts will soon be with us. Enjoy the Willow Warbler's tinkling cadence, the Blackcap's rich fruity warbling and even the Chiffchaff's monotonous "zip, zap." Spring is here!

First published in *Bedfordshire County Life Magazine* in spring 2002

Wildlife Puzzle 2

Q. One former name of a bird, with strange appearance and strange behaviour, was Cuckoo's Mate, because it arrived in Britain in early April, at about the same time as the Cuckoo. What word, still in common English usage, is derived from that bird's even older name, because it used to be trapped and used in magic to effect the return of a lover or to cast a spell on an enemy?

Of voles, squirrels and dandelions

I have just been looking for Water Voles. Without success. This charming mammal – 'Rattie' in Kenneth Grahame's *The Wind in the Willows* – used to be common along the rivers Ivel and Great Ouse, but is now a rare sight. Escaped or released alien North American Minks, now living ferally and preying upon our native amphibians, birds and mammals, have been blamed. There have been both national and local surveys to establish the facts, and to discover sites where Water Voles can still be found. Professional conservationists (such as Amanda Proud for the Ivel Valley Countryside Project) have provided training for amateur volunteer surveyors, who have been searching the banks of rivers, streams and ditches for the tell-tale signs of Water Vole activity, including vole-sized holes, runways, nibbled grass tips, little stacks of cut grass, and neat latrines. Very well organised, these Water Voles! Actually *seeing* a Water Vole is a real bonus. If you have seen one anywhere along the River Ivel, the River Great Ouse or any other local waterway recently, and can recall the exact location and the date, please report it to the Bedfordshire Natural History Society's mammal recorder (at mammals@bnhs.org.uk).

Another North American alien that creates havoc at this time of year is the Grey Squirrel. I can watch them from my study window as they traverse and search the hedgerows, looking for the nests of Song Thrushes, Blackbirds, Chaffinches and Long-tailed Tits, which they raid, eating the eggs and nestlings. I do not mind them stealing the nuts and seeds that I put out for birds, or even raiding my fruit trees in autumn, and they can look very attractive as they scamper across the lawn, but I do draw the line when they pick up a live nestling and nibble at it, like a child eating an ice-cream. They are not part of our native fauna, and are vermin, so far as I am concerned, fully deserving their nickname of 'Tree Rats'.

I am not, however, wholly anti aliens, and welcome some additions to our countryside, such as the charming and benign Little Owl, which consumes mostly beetles and earthworms, and Bedfordshire's most spectacular bird, the exotic and elusive Lady Amherst's Pheasant.

We all have favourite birds, mammals or plants, but also our individual pet hates. I have often wondered why it is that I protect and nurture the Primroses and Cowslips on a bank in my garden, leaving the grass uncut around them, so that they flourish and seed successfully, yet instantly remove any Dandelion that dares to show its equally (if not more) attractive flowers. This must be derived from my upbringing, generations of British gardeners having eradicated Dandelions from their immaculate lawns. But why? In many Continental countries, Dandelions are grown, blanched, and used as highly regarded salad plants, and there are many Bedfordshire roundabouts that are as beautiful with their wild Dandelions in May as they were with their carefully planted Crocuses in March and Daffodils in April.

But what is beauty? One late spring day, I was driving near Ridgmont when, in the distance, my companion and I spotted a wonderful flower-covered bank. The grass was smothered with splashes of colour: red, yellow, blue, orange, violet and white amongst the green. Absolutely beautiful! Then, as we got closer, we realised that the splashes of colour were not wild flowers, but were plastic bags, discarded crisp packets and other rubbish, blown from a nearby tip. Admired beauty turned instantly to abhorred ugliness. Margaret Hungerford wrote, and we all remember the quotation, that "Beauty is in the eye of the beholder", but David Hume, writing a century earlier, was less poetic, but more accurate, when he said "Beauty in things exists in the mind which contemplates them."

Don't forget to report those Water Voles.

First published in *Bedfordshire County Life Magazine* in summer 2002

Wildlife Puzzle 3

Q. Where in Bedfordshire could you see from far away a white example of an animal that links Peter, Susan, Edmund and Lucy with a dangerous coral-dwelling fish and a clock?

Wildlife Puzzle 4

Q. The name of which sporting freshwater fish combines elements from (1) a black, white and red butterfly whose caterpillars feed on stinging nettles, (2) a springtime butterfly related to the whites, whose males are much more colourful than the females, (3) a bunting said to sing "A little bit of bread and no cheese", (4) a bird that was a professor in *Bagpuss*, (5) the wild endymion, (6) a North American bunting, and (7) Piglet's favourite flower?

Shades of summer

It is always interesting to be in the presence of an expert and to listen, look and learn. I have taken the opportunity to do this several times this year, by taking part in field meetings run by the Bedfordshire Natural History Society. As a result, I have watched delicate and elegant Wood White butterflies along woodland rides, and Dark Green Fritillary butterflies sunning themselves and then swooping away over chalk downland. I have been shown the rare Greater Pignut and the strange brown-and-cream, saprophytic chlorophyll-less Yellow Bird's-nest, both plants which I would have walked straight past (and probably trodden on) if I had not been with an expert. The Society has a field trip almost every week throughout the year, the themes varying from Badger-watching and learning to identify bats with an electronic bat-detector, to finding and naming shield-bugs, fungi or lichens, night-time moth studies and birdwatching trips. The ambling walks in friendly company are informal, and there is usually a mid-morning picnic-break, when the experts are happy to answer even the most naive of questions. If you are sufficiently interested to be reading this text, you will certainly benefit by joining the BNHS and you can have a 'trial run', since the Society stresses that "non-members are always welcome" on its field trips. If you would like details, visit the Society's website, www.bnhs.org.uk

Rattie found! In the last article, I reported that amateur naturalists were out searching for the rapidly vanishing Water Vole ("Rattie" in Kenneth Grahame's *The Wind in the Willows*), and that I had myself been out looking for evidence of this little mammal, but had been unsuccessful. Scarcely had this been printed than I did find 'suspicious-looking' holes and nibbled grass tips along a little brook. The Ivel Valley Countryside Project Water Vole Survey's professional organiser, Amanda Proud, came to check, and she declared that I had indeed discovered a small, but thriving population of Water Voles. My emotion was relief (that I had not called her out on a wild goose chase); hers I can only describe as elation. If you see a Water Vole in the county or have reason to suspect that they are present, contact the BNHS's mammal recorder at mammals@bnhs.org.uk

Birdwatchers always get excited about rarities, and this summer's highlight was a completely unexpected Razorbill that turned up at Radwell on a calm day in June. These days, there seem to be frequent panic headlines about a catastrophic decline in numbers of what is claimed to be the latest 'doomed' species (Song Thrush and Sky Lark were named recently). This year, however, two of our summer visitors certainly do seem to have arrived in much reduced numbers. How many Cuckoos have you heard this year? Not many is my guess. Instead of several every day from mid April until the end of June, I have heard the male's "cuck-oo" only 21 times this year, and, for the first year in my life, I have not heard the female's bubbling song at all.

The second summer visitor to have been unusually scarce this year is the plainly plumaged but engaging Spotted Flycatcher. Perching upright on a prominent bare twig, fence or wire, the 'Spot Fly' swoops out, catches a fly with aerobatic expertise and, usually, returns to the same perch. Its song is scarcely a song at all, merely a few scratchy squeaks, but those lucky enough to have Spotted Flycatchers in their garden usually know them and love them, since they can be almost as confiding as are Robins, and often nest in ivy or other creepers on the walls of the house, and readily use nest-boxes put up for Robins. They do not stay long with us, usually arriving in the first few days of May and departing in August (though migrants, probably from Scandinavia, may be seen as late as October), but they came late this year, the first in Bedfordshire not being observed until 16th May, and in small numbers. As well as large gardens, a favourite habitat is churchyards, where there are usually mature trees, open 'glades' and plenty of perches (tombstones are ideal!). Many Bedfordshire birders have, therefore, been out this summer, looking in the local churchyards, checking on the presence or absence of breeding Spotted Flycatchers. By checking again in future years, it will be possible to see whether the numbers of this enchanting species are recovering or still declining.

While visiting over 30 of Bedfordshire's churchyards, I became aware of the number of carefully maintained gravestones, dating back to 1939-45, dedicated to British, American, Canadian, Polish and other airmen. As I sat on one bench, quietly watching and listening for the give-away calls of a Spotted Flycatcher, I read the plaque on the seat and shall now pass on to you its poignant message:

When you go home - Tell them of us and say,
"For your tomorrow - We gave our today."

First published in *Bedfordshire County Life Magazine* in autumn 2002

Mellow fruitfulness

In a lifetime stretching back to the early 1940s, I cannot remember another year in which the bushes and trees in the countryside have been so covered with fruit. The autumn of 2002 will surely go down in history as a phenomenal season for this natural harvest? The Bramble bushes have been covered with succulent blackberries, eaten by warblers and thrushes, picked bare by human blackberry-pickers, and then within a few days providing yet another crop. The Elder trees have been weighed down with their bunches of juicy black elderberries. The Blackthorn bushes have been covered with sharp-tasting dull-blue sloes. Some Crab-apple trees have been so covered in fruit that the leaves and branches have been scarcely visible. The Hawthorn trees glow red with haws, the briars of Wild Rose are smothered with glossy hips, and the Horse Chestnut trees keep schoolchildren happy with abundant conkers.

"It's a sure sign of a hard winter to come," I have been informed pessimistically by the local sage. More likely, it is an indication of weather past rather than weather future, especially the mild early spring, when the blossom was not frosted.

This year there is plenty of food for the hordes of winter visitors – migrant thrushes such as Redwings and Fieldfares and finches such as Bramblings from northern Europe – but we have yet to see whether they reach us in large numbers. If the autumn harvest is as abundant farther north and east as it is in Bedfordshire, they may tarry to feed elsewhere. The largest arrivals of some species come when, following a productive breeding season, food is in short supply, and wandering migrants travel farther west than usual in search of food. There was a spectacular example of this in 1983, when the acorn crop failed and Jays – which feed largely on acorns in autumn and winter – moved westwards in Britain in search of food. In west Cornwall, where Jays are usually scarce, over 1,000 were seen on six days in October, and there were some 2,000 in just one area on one day, including 800 in a single field. This will not happen this year, with many Oak trees laden with acorns, but, if the crop fails next year, who knows? Similarly, it is the years when food farther east is in short supply that we get the big influxes of Bohemian Waxwings, and can enjoy watching these colourful birds feeding on *Cotoneaster* berries in our parks and gardens. Last winter, there was a small but much-watched flock near the roundabout on the A421 just south of Kempston. Even if you did not see the birds, perhaps you saw the throngs of *Barbour*-jacketed, telescope-toting twitchers along the roadside verges?

Not long ago, the advice from environmentalists was that gardens should be planted up with native British bushes and trees, with alien plants given short shrift. Now, however, it is realised that the exotic plants that make our gardens and parks so colourful also act as insurance for our wildlife. In productive years, such as 2002, there are plenty of berries and nuts on the native bushes and trees, but, in years when these are scarce, birds and mammals can turn to the fruits of foreign ornamental plants. This may even be one of the reasons that some birds, such as Blackcaps, now increasingly overwinter in Britain, whereas they were formerly only summer visitors here.

Gardens are important as wildlife habitat even if they are not managed especially for wildlife (as many are these days). The current fashion for 'designer gardens', promoted by some television programmes, is doubtless wonderful news for garden centres selling rocks, gravel and paving, but is definitely very bad news for Hedgehogs, Frogs, voles, butterflies and birds. Even a tiny lawn is full of life, and the invertebrates provide food for wild birds and mammals. It seems such a shame that, as our country becomes increasingly covered in the tarmac and concrete of roads and buildings, many of the oases that were our gardens are now also being destroyed, just to satisfy a short-lived, commercially inspired fashion.

If you dig a pond or plant a berry-bearing bush or fragrant flower, you will get far more enjoyment from watching its visitors than you will ever get from barren concrete or wood chippings. Those of us who do still have real gardens also know that a little bit of untidiness can be a big help to wildlife. A log left to rot away naturally provides a home for many creatures, and a pile of leaves in a corner could be a warm winter haven for a Hedgehog and a nursery for another generation.

If you would like to help in recording natural wildlife events, such as fruiting changes from year to year, visit www.woodlandtrust.org.uk or write to The Woodland Trust, Autumn Park, Dysart Road, Grantham, Lincolnshire NG31 6LL. If you would like a free booklet about gardening for wildlife, visit www.birdfood.co.uk or write to CJ WildBird Foods, The Rea, Upton Magna, Shrewsbury SY4 4UR.

First published in *Bedfordshire County Life Magazine* in winter 2002/03

Can spring be far behind?

The abundance of berries last autumn did provide a suitable welcome for a few small flocks of immigrant Bohemian Waxwings in the county, notably half a dozen that fed among customers' cars at the St Neots *Tesco* store just over the border in Cambridgeshire, but which flew into Bedfordshire to roost overnight at the RSPB's headquarters at Sandy.

In some years, the 'winter thrushes' (Redwings and Fieldfares from Scandinavia and farther east) almost desert the county by late winter, when the ground is frozen and the berries have been eaten, but this year there were big flocks still to be seen on old pasture and in the hedgerows.

The heavy rainfall that created severe floods – the worst for some 60 years in some places – was unwelcome to most people, but did have at least one benefit for wildlife. The valley of the River Great Ouse was converted into a series of huge lakes, with floating weed seeds concentrated like the wrack along the tide line on the coast. This provided wonderful feeding areas for dabbling ducks, diving ducks, geese, swans, plovers, snipe and other assorted wildfowl and waders. Their wheeling flocks and evocative cries made inland Bedfordshire look and sound like The Wash or the North Kent Marshes, to the delight of local birdwatchers. The waterlogged fields alongside the floods created unusual conditions for exuberant 'Mad March' Hares, chasing each other and producing huge splashes, much to the amusement of human onlookers. When cold conditions followed the floods, places that were usually ploughed fields suddenly became free skating rinks for local schoolchildren. It was a winter to remember.

The first signs of spring were apparent as early as January, with Snowdrops in sheltered spots. Mistle Thrushes gave voice to their clear, fluty notes, audible above motorway noise or the roar of a winter gale, hence their old country name of 'Storm Cocks'. They can be nest-building in early February and be sitting on eggs in a nest decorated with snow by the end of the month. This year, Hazel catkins were out, and Chaffinches and Song Thrushes were singing in early February, clearly having decided that, in the warm spring-like weather, it was indeed spring. They must have been taken by surprise, as were the region's motorists, when the blizzards came.

It is in late winter and early spring that the woodpeckers start their breeding activities. All it needs is a bright sunny morning, even if there is a heavy frost on the ground, and Great Spotted Woodpeckers can be heard 'drumming'. They are, contrary to popular opinion, not excavating their nest holes, but are, by mechanical means rather than vocally, sending out the same messages as the singing thrushes: "I'm here. This is my territory." It is simultaneously an invitation to a potential mate and a warning to a rival to keep away. A couple of decades ago, the weaker drumming of the Lesser Spotted Woodpecker was also heard not uncommonly, but the smallest of our woodpeckers (the size of a sparrow, with a barred back) is now very scarce in Bedfordshire. Why? The reason is a bit of a mystery, for its larger pied relative is now much commoner, and so too is the even larger Green Woodpecker.

Although some birds, such as Ringed Plovers and Redshanks, largely absent in winter from our part of England, may reappear in February and March, the first 'real' migrants (those that overwinter to the south of Britain) do not generally appear until the end of March and early April. A few Chiffchaffs brave our winter climate, but the monotonous "zip-zap" song from bare-twigged branches above flowering Primroses in almost every little coppice or wood is usually the first sign that summer really is just around the corner. The buzzing calls of Sand Martins, looking like small, brown, short-tailed swallows as they skim over a lake or flooded gravel-pit or clay-pit, usually precede the first genuine Barn Swallows (to give them their full official English name) that are taken as *the* sign of the arrival of spring. The first ones should be here by now.

First published in *Bedfordshire County Life Magazine* in spring 2003

Wildlife Puzzle 5

Q. Identify the four Bedfordshire villages suggested by these clues:
(1) On heaths, it resembles benign furze, gorse or whin, but up high the witches' version is caused by mites; (2) Acorn producer before the recently sown meadow; (3) Site often considered by environmentalists to be unsuitable for development; (4) Ale goes down this, it's cross when shaded, but addled eggs don't.
Now join 1 to 2 and join 3 to 4. What six-letter word starting with T and ending with R might one expect to be produced where these lines cross?
(Use of an Ordnance Survey map is recommended.)

Of cranes and cuckoos

27°C one day, and 4°C the next. Spring was strange this year.

But we seem to say that about almost every season recently, with warm winters, cold summers, droughts and floods, and heat-waves or cold snaps when we least expect them. If that is confusing for us, with our centrally heated and air-conditioned offices and cars, imagine how disruptive of routine activities it must be for wildlife. A warm sunny day on 21st February brought forth from hibernation a Small Tortoiseshell butterfly to delight me at South Mills near Sandy, and on the same day Tony Ploszajski saw a Peacock butterfly over the A421 near Brogborough. A mite early!

It was a spring to put smiles on the faces of many Bedfordshire birdwatchers, and also twitchers who came from neighbouring counties. In one purple patch, it seemed that rare birds were being discovered in the county almost every other day. The highlight was a little flock of Common Cranes that took up residence for a few days in March at West Hyde, southeast of Luton. Almost a quarter as big again as a Grey Heron, five of these elegant birds strode around among Lapwings, Carrion Crows and Golden Plovers, feeding, preening and mildly displaying in the middle of a large field, and easily viewable from the nearby minor road.

The earliest spring migrants appeared on cue in reasonable numbers, but, despite the summer-like weather, the later migrants were slow to arrive, with just a scattering instead of the expected widespread reports. By the end of April, when the woods should have been echoing with the songs of Cuckoos and the purring of Turtle Doves, many birdwatchers had still not heard either. The arrival of

Cuckoos has been getting later and later every year, and in the past two or three years the decline in numbers has been very noticeable. Why? To be frank, nobody knows. The Cuckoo's diet consists almost wholly of insects, especially large caterpillars and beetles, including many of those large hairy caterpillars that are avoided by other birds. One would think that global warming would have been beneficial to large insects and, if Cuckoos were arriving earlier and in larger numbers than usual, this would have been a convenient explanation. After all, the insect-eating Hobby has increased in numbers, and this tiny migrant falcon is now far more widespread in summer in Bedfordshire than it was even twenty years ago. Why have Cuckoos not reacted in the same way? Presumably, something nasty is happening to them in their African wintering grounds or on migration. Much research may be needed to discover the reason, for such declines (and increases) among animals and plants involve many interactions between species and responses to a whole range of environmental factors. There is often no simple answer. The fact, however, is that Cuckoos are few and far between. Last year, I did not hear a single female Cuckoo in Bedfordshire (her bubbling song is quite different from the male's "cuck-oo"), and this year I did not hear my first male until 1st May. If you have heard one this year, count yourself lucky. This bird's song was so much a part of the English summer that William Shakespeare wrote "… as the Cuckoo is in June, heard but not regarded." Nowadays, we should pay heed to every one, and hope that this epitome of a summer's day does not go the way of the Wryneck, once known as 'the Cuckoo's mate' since it arrived here at about the same time in spring, but now long extinct as a breeding bird in England.

Cuckoos may be scarce, but there is lots of good news to compensate. Have you recently noticed a large bird of prey circling overhead, its broad wings slightly raised above the horizontal? It is quite likely that you have, for Common Buzzards have now become widespread in Bedfordshire, with a pair or two nesting in many of the county's woods. It is not unusual these days to see more Common Buzzards than Kestrels on a walk or a drive in the countryside. Yet until just a few years ago Common Buzzards were known only in winter, and had not nested here for 100 years. Their favourite prey is Rabbits, which makes them popular with farmers. With luck, we may also soon be able to see Red Kites here. A few wander into the county now and again, and some have stayed for a while even in summer. The re-establishment experiments in Oxfordshire and Northamptonshire have been very successful, but the spread into neighbouring counties seems slow. [Just four years after this was written, Red Kites were breeding in Bedfordshire.] They can apparently find plenty of food where they are, so the populations become denser and denser rather than expanding. Since they feed almost wholly on carrion, especially dead Rabbits, they too are popular with farmers. Look out for a large and elegant bird of prey with chestnut-brown plumage, long wings and a long deeply forked tail that is twisted and turned in flight like a rudder as the bird performs agile aerobatics. With the possibility of occasional migrant Honey-buzzard, Marsh Harrier, Montagu's Harrier, Goshawk, Osprey and Red-footed Falcon in summer (and Peregrine Falcon, Merlin and Hen Harrier in winter), breeding Kestrels, Sparrowhawks, Hobbies and Common Buzzards, and a few wandering Red Kites, it is theoretically possible to notch up ten species of bird of prey in

Bedfordshire in a day. Four in a day is now commonplace, and five relatively unremarkable. Who would have thought that possible when, back in the 'Pesticide Era' of the 1960s, only the Kestrel could still be seen regularly, and there were only three confirmed breeding records of Sparrowhawk in the county in a whole ten-year period? Now that you can, revel in the raptors!

First published in *Bedfordshire County Life Magazine* in summer 2003

Wildlife Puzzle 6

Q. Which name is left over after you have paired up eight old country names with their eight modern names? Match (1) "The Grand Surprise", (2) "Jack Go To Bed At Noon", (3) "Lady with Twelve Flounces", (4) "Watchman of the Marshes", (5) "Urchin", (6) "Weasel Duck", (7) "Weasel's Snout", (8) "Wet my Lips", and (9) "Whistler" with (a) Quail, (b) Redshank, (c) Wigeon, (d) Goat's-beard, (e) Goldfinch, (f) Hedgehog, (g) Lesser Snapdragon, and (h) Smew.

Wildlife Puzzle 7

Q. Which king, the son of a reputed arachnologist, is brought to mind by a famous inhabitant of Woburn, named in honour of a French missionary, a sotto voce presenter who graduated from Cambridge University and gambolled with Gorillas, and a teetotal vegetarian who died on 1st March?

Painted Ladies and Thorn-apples

The wonderful thing about natural history is that a walk anywhere – in the town as well as in the country – can spring surprises.

In June this year, I took up a long-standing invitation to stay for a few days with my old friend Robert Gillmor, the famous bird artist, and his equally talented wife Sue, at their home on the Norfolk coast. We planned to have some relaxed birdwatching, but on the first afternoon, just as I had arrived, they told me about the Hummingbird Hawk-moth that had appeared the previous evening, feeding at Red Valerian flowers in their garden. I was most envious, since I had seen that delightful species several times in Ireland in October, but not for some years and never in England. As we sat sipping our drinks, no hawk-moth appeared, but the flowers in their garden were visited by a number of Painted Lady butterflies, and it was clear that 2003 was going to be a 'good year' for this migrant species. During my stay, Robert and I saw up to a hundred or so Painted Ladies every day, and we even found a second Hummingbird Hawk-moth, feeding at flowers on the cliff-top at Weybourne.

Both of these insects occur here almost exclusively as migrants (from North Africa and southern Europe), though a few Hummingbird Hawk-moths may occasionally overwinter as adults in southwest England. Most are, therefore, seen in coastal areas when they have recently arrived, as with the ones that Robert Gillmor and I watched in Norfolk. They do, however, filter inland, and good numbers of Painted Ladies have occurred this year in Bedfordshire, where – along with Small Tortoiseshells, Red Admirals, Peacocks and Commas

– they especially delight in visiting the flowers of *Buddleia*, the so-called Butterfly Bush, where they provide delight for us.

The Painted Lady is beautiful, as its name suggests, but perhaps no more so than the other butterflies that come to *Buddleia*. The origin of its name is obscure, but this butterfly was once referred to as *Papilio Bella Donna*, and an extract of belladonna ('beautiful lady', the Deadly Nightshade) was formerly used in ladies' cosmetics, as the poison atropine enlarges the pupils, giving an appealing, wide-eyed appearance.

The Hummingbird Hawk-moth typically zips back and forth from flower to flower, then hovers with whirring wings as its long proboscis seeks nectar from deep within the corolla-tube. Its name is very appropriate, since it looks so much like a hummingbird that people unfamiliar with it are often quite insistent that they have seen the bird (which does not occur in Europe outside zoo collections) and not an insect. The key identification features, apart from its behaviour, are orange on the hind wings and black-and-white marks on the end of the 'tail' (the rear end of the abdomen). Several have been noted, almost always singly, in Bedfordshire this year. In August, when botanising, with Chris Boon and Judy Knight from the Bedfordshire Natural History Society, I was very pleased to find one feeding at Honeysuckle in West Wood near Souldrop.

It has been an exceptional year in Britain for both of these species, though numbers will probably turn out to have been fewer than the peaks in 1947 (when over 1,000 Hummingbird Hawk-moths were reported) and 1996 (the recent bumper year for Painted Ladies, when 'many millions' occurred here).

Thus, these butterfly and moth discoveries came unexpectedly, when the primary objectives were birds and plants. Similarly, the most interesting plant discovery came when Dave Odell, [then] the county Bird Recorder, and I were looking for migrant wading birds and waterfowl at Broom. There, growing in a field of Potatoes, were hundreds of Thorn-apple plants, some only a few inches high, but others coming up to my waist. Most had long, attractive, trumpet-shaped white flowers, and some had their spiky green fruits well developed, ranging in size from that of a conker to that of a small fist. I had never seen this weird plant before, yet suddenly we had come across 800 or more in a single field.

The Thorn-apple is poisonous and is related to other poisonous plants such as Henbane and Deadly Nightshade, but also to the Potato and Tomato. Its origin is not known, but it may be native to the New World or to the Black Sea area. It occurs here mainly as a 'wool alien', its seeds being transported in sheep's wool that is spread on the land to improve soil quality.

Thus, you never know what you are going to find, and it's often something that you least expect. A walk on your own can be fun, but a walk with an expert is even better. The Bedfordshire Natural History Society welcomes not only new members, but also interested non-members on its almost-weekly field trips, led by the county's top experts in everything from birds to mosses and from fungi to mammals. For details, visit the Society's website at www.bnhs.org.uk

First published in *Bedfordshire County Life Magazine* in autumn 2003

Leaf-fall

The autumn that has just passed was notable for its prolonged and beautiful leaf colours, enhanced by the unseasonably brilliant sunshine on many days. After the 'long, hot summer of 2003' – which will doubtless remain in our memories like that of 1976, unless such summers become the norm – with scarcely any rain for weeks on end, many trees seem to have reacted by retaining their leaves for longer than usual and by fruiting profusely. We have benefited by their wonderful hues. Ash and Hawthorn give the appearance of having suffered most, with leaves shrivelled on the trees, but ash keys and hawthorn haws still hang in great clusters.

Wildlife in general must have suffered in the dry days of summer, for earthworms will have burrowed deep, making life difficult for Moles, Hedgehogs, Red Foxes, Badgers, Wood Mice, Little Owls and the like. The abundant fruits of autumn will, however, suddenly have made life very easy for Grey Squirrels, mice and thrushes. Whatever the weather, there are winners and losers among plants and among the animals that depend upon them (and among the animals that depend upon those animals).

The period of leaf-fall always reminds me of a unique experience far from Bedfordshire. In one October in the early 1970s, I was staying in the foothills of the Carpathian Mountains in eastern Poland. It had been a mild autumn and the hoped-for bird migration was not taking place, for the days were damp and the nights and dawns were foggy. One night, however, the sky cleared, bringing with it a heavy frost. In the morning, every leaf on every tree was covered not just with frost, but with layers of ice, glistening in the first sunshine for days. Overhead, the sky was filled with migrating birds. Held up for days by the fog, with its clearance they all headed south. Tens if not hundreds of thousands of Rooks, Jackdaws, Crows, Cranes, thrushes, finches, buntings, larks and pipits, together with hundreds of hawks and scores of eagles and owls, all pouring through a gap between the peaks of the Carpathians. That was fantastic, fabulous and exciting enough, but what accompanied it was just as memorable. Until that day, there had been almost no leaf-fall in the calm, mild autumn, but, as the sun warmed up the leaves, heavy with ice, they began to fall. Every single one fell, all within a period of just a couple of hours. On this calm, clear, frosty morning, with the sky filled with migrating birds, this sudden leaf-fall created an unbelievable roar, as loud perhaps as that in the middle of a busy motorway. A once-in-a-lifetime experience.

Having digressed from Bedfordshire's wildlife already, perhaps I may be forgiven for continuing on the theme of memorable wildlife occasions. The top ten in my lifetime would also include eye-to-eye contact with Mountain Gorillas in Rwanda; a cruising Whale Shark (the World's largest fish) swimming below and dwarfing our yacht in the Indian Ocean; touching Grey Whales (and again having eye-to-eye contact with a 'Great Beast') in Mexico, with the whales chasing us to do so, since they wanted it as much as we did; and my first-ever sighting of a pod of Killer Whales off Western Ireland, when I at first misidentified the male's huge dorsal fin as the periscope of a submarine. Every occasion on which I have snorkelled over a coral reef, in the Red Sea or the Andaman Sea, has been a magical experience, like entering a brilliantly coloured fairyland. Another fairyland is to be found in the temperate rainforests of

Fjordland in the south of South Island in New Zealand. It was there is the 1980s that a Swedish professor came up to me and said "Ah, it is as if Tolkien had been here," an apt comment as we stood transfixed among the exquisitely lush mosses and ferns, and also prophetic, since this was, years later, chosen as the location for filming *The Lord of the Rings* trilogy.

Ornithologically, I shall never forget the tit irruption of 1957, when thousands of Blue, Great and Coal Tits crossed the English Channel and the North Sea. I was at Sandwich Bay in Kent when hundreds arrived, exhausted from their journey, and rested on branches, the bare ground, windowsills, roofs, and even my shoulders, and tiny bodies of those that did not quite make it were washed up on the shoreline. Huge numbers of migrating birds are seen regularly at a few special sites around the World. In Britain, Fair Isle between Orkney and Shetland, Spurn in Yorkshire, and Dungeness in Kent are perhaps the three best known (the Isles of Scilly are famous for rare birds and for large numbers of birdwatchers, not for large numbers of birds), but all are eclipsed by Heligoland, the tiny island in the corner of the North Sea between Denmark, Germany and the Netherlands, that is a resting place for migrant song-birds on their way from Scandinavia, Finland and Russia to southern Europe and Africa. A week there one October is another highlight among my wildlife experiences. It was there that I saw more Siskins in one day than I had seen in the whole of the rest of my life, and one grassy field held so many Song Thrushes and Robins that they were all just a metre or so apart, evenly spaced as if they were pieces on a draughtboard.

My tenth and final memorable lifetime experience concerns a group of five huge birds which four of us saw flying out into the Atlantic from the southernmost point of Ireland at midday on 1st September 1965, in brilliant sunshine when the sea was mirror-calm. Never closer than a mile away, but still visible at a range of over five miles, we never succeeded in identifying them for certain, but the best guess in retrospect, first suggested by Dr Cliff Henty, is that they were a group of Griffon Vultures that had soared away from the Spanish or Portuguese coast on a thermal the day before, had found themselves far out to sea over the Bay of Biscay or the Western Approaches, and were attempting to make their way back to Iberia. The full story has been told in print elsewhere, but it remains a mystery to this day.

Back in Bedfordshire, anyone wanting to see an amazing sight at this time of year should go to Marston Vale towards dusk to watch thousands of gulls flying in to roost safely for the night on the waters at Stewartby. That is our own local 'ornithological spectacular'.

First published in *Bedfordshire County Life Magazine* in winter 2003/04

Wildlife Puzzle 8

Q. You find a tall perennial plant with beautiful blue flowers in long spikes, a small, extremely common weed with heart-shaped seed pods, and a spiny evergreen bush that seems to have many small green leaves (but doesn't!). From among the shopkeeper, the cleric and the stockman, who cleans up, who protects his money and who has no need for a hat?

Wildlife Puzzle 9

Q. If you came across an ancient mariner, a punctuation mark, a collector of tolls, part of the hairstyle of a nice girl of the roving kind, and the pinnacle of the British ruling classes, which of the five would you be most excited to have discovered in Bedfordshire?

Tiny woodpeckers and rare tits

With spring upon us, the countryside seems to wake up, with Primroses in the hedgerows, the buzz of bees and the sound of birdsong everywhere.

The Bedfordshire Bird Club has launched a special survey this spring to discover the current status in Bedfordshire of two declining species: Lesser Spotted Woodpecker and Willow Tit.

Twenty or thirty years ago, these two birds were widespread, but both are now scarce enough in the county for most birdwatchers to note every one that they see or hear and to report them to the county recorder at the end of the year. These casual observations are valuable, but the aim of this year's survey is to encourage observers actively to seek these species not only in all the known sites (where they have been recorded in the past ten years), but also in new sites, and to put the records in context by also recording related species.

Birdwatchers will be visiting suitable areas of woodland (including shelterbelts, copses and lines of riverside trees) from now until July, noting not only any Lesser Spotted Woodpecker and Willow Tit, but also every observation of the commoner and closely related Great Spotted Woodpecker, Green Woodpecker and Marsh Tit.

A mere 30 years ago, Lesser Spotted Woodpeckers were only slightly less widespread in Bedfordshire than were the other two woodpecker species, being recorded in 73 sites in the county, compared with 117 for Green Woodpecker and 119 for Great Spotted Woodpecker. At that time, Willow Tits were also almost as frequent as Marsh Tits (found in 107 and 122 sites, respectively), and in the previous decade may even have been the commoner of the two. How different it is now! The woodpecker is known from only about ten sites and the tit from less than half a dozen.

By collecting the records of all five species, the relative numbers will give an indication of the extent of coverage of each woodland area. In addition, who knows what changes there may be in the *next* 30 years? Green Woodpecker and Great Spotted Woodpecker have both greatly increased in numbers and expanded their ranges within Bedfordshire in recent years. Once typical only of the woodland on the county's greensand ridge, they have extended now throughout the lowlands of the river valleys. In the future, they may further increase, or alternatively crash back to their former status. Marsh Tits have apparently declined recently, though to a far lesser extent than have Willow Tits. That situation could, however, seesaw. Only time will tell.

The Bird Club's aim is to take a 'snapshot' of the current situation in Bedfordshire's woodlands, by means of this very simple survey. Willow and Marsh Tits have several subtle differences in their plumages and calls, but are very difficult to tell apart.

Most people know the Green Woodpecker, with its bright green plumage, yellow rump, red crown and laughing call – the well-known yaffle, after which Professor Yaffle of *Bagpuss* fame was named. It is most often seen either feeding on ants on a lawn or grassy field, or flying away with undulating flight towards the nearest area of trees.

The Great Spotted Woodpecker is smaller – the size of a Blackbird rather than the size of a Collared Dove – and is strikingly black-and-white, with bright pink under its tail and, on males and juveniles, but not females, some bright red on its head.

The Lesser Spotted Woodpecker is, like the Great Spotted, black-and-white, but never has pink under its tail, and only the male has any red (on its crown). It is, however, exceedingly distinct, for it is not the size of a Collared Dove, or a Blackbird, but is absolutely tiny – no bigger than a sparrow.

Although the Lesser Spotted Woodpecker is now so rare (only a very few are known in Bedfordshire), it can nest in gardens, in parks, in trees alongside a river – indeed, almost anywhere. If you suspect that you may have seen one (or even better a pair), the Bedfordshire Bird Club would like to hear from you (visit www.bedsbirdclub.org.uk).

Lesser Spotted Woodpeckers may start drumming and singing on calm, dry, sunny days in January and February, even when there is a sharp frost or snow on the ground. With bare trees, observation at this time and in early spring is far easier than it is in summer when the trees are in full leaf.

Woodpeckers announce their territories by rapid taps with their bill on a 'sounding-board', usually a dead branch. This 'drumming' is quite different from the tapping when they (or other birds such as Nuthatches or Great Tits) are extracting insects from a piece of wood or bark. Green Woodpeckers seldom drum, but they do do so occasionally. Great Spotted Woodpeckers frequently drum, and may use different sounding boards, making very different noises. Since both sexes drum, duetting is not infrequent, and can sound like two different species. The drumming of Lesser Spotted Woodpecker, however, is very different from that of Great Spotted Woodpecker. Each burst of drumming by the smaller species lasts almost twice as long (an average of 25 strikes per series lasting 1.2 seconds, compared with an average of 13 strikes per series lasting 0.6 seconds), is quieter or 'weaker', is higher-pitched, and, diagnostically, is *even* (with equal spaces between each strike), whereas that of Great Spotted always accelerates towards the end (with shorter gaps between each strike) and often becomes quieter just before ceasing. The Lesser Spotted Woodpecker also has a distinctive song – "pee-pee-pee-pee ..." – similar to those of Nuthatch and Kestrel, which is never given by its larger relative.

With these clues, do *you* have Lesser Spotted Woodpeckers at the bottom of *your* garden?

First published in *Bedfordshire County Life Magazine* in spring 2004

Wildlife Puzzle 10

Q. A chart to find your way, a container for an old salt's effects, what's left after someone's gone, and after a fire, the end of a balloon, a honey-maker, and a feature both of a cow and of a car. Which of the seven is the only one that is not unfinished?

Wildlife Puzzle 11

Q. On walks in Bedfordshire, you found three plants. On sandy soil, one was small, with long-stalked leaves at the base, but one pair completely encircling the stem, and small, five-petalled white flowers. In dry grassland, you were delighted to find a small orchid with tiny white flowers arranged spirally in a single row up the spike. Finally, you re-found a small plant - not seen in Bedfordshire since 1878 – with a rosette of rounded leaves and very pale pinkish globular flowers in a stalked spike. Which season is missing?

You never know what you'll find

This spring, I have visited over one hundred woods in Bedfordshire, making counts of Marsh Tits and each of the three species of British woodpecker (and hoping to find a Willow Tit) for the Bedfordshire Bird Club's 2004 survey of these five species, described in the previous article.

What a variety of woodland we have – ancient dry oakwoods with carpets of bluebells, dense plantations of larch, spruce or pine, hazel coppice, poplar plantations, bare-floored beechwoods, wet birch and alder carr, mixed-woodland spinneys preserved for the benefit of Pheasants – all shown as green patches on the maps, their nature apparent only when they are visited in person. Every visit to a wood is an exciting trip of discovery.

My visits to look for woodpeckers and tits have been enormously enlivened by the unexpected finds, not only of birds, but also of plants and insects. It has been a wonderful spring for blossom, following last year's marvellous summer and with no really hard frosts in winter to destroy the buds. With some hot spring days, the early butterflies have taken full advantage. How can one not delight in seeing glowing Small Tortoiseshells and Commas, 'bright-eyed' Peacocks, brilliant yellow Brimstones and flitting Orange-tips on a sunny spring morning with the trees still bare of leaves and dew on the grass?

Since – like most birds – woodpeckers are more active and vocal in the early morning, I have been going out early, often taking my breakfast with me and eating it in the wood that I am surveying. As a result (apart from feeling exhausted by the afternoon!), I have often come across grazing deer that do not expect to find a human being abroad at such hours. In our county, the most common by far is the Muntjac, now well established over much of southern England, but originating from China via Woburn Park. Also known as the Barking Deer, its sudden dog-like bark is heard even more often than the scream of a vixen or yelp of a dog Fox. Increasingly widespread in the county is another ex-Woburn escapee, the Chinese Water Deer. The Muntjac superficially resembles a large Rabbit more than a deer (despite its little horns and tusks), with its high rear end and head-downwards dash away in panic, with white tail flying, when disturbed. The Chinese Water Deer, on the other hand, is an elegant beast. It stands alert, with a long neck, large rounded ears pricked, and black eyes and black nose prominent as three dark dots, contrasting with its generally pale, sandy-coloured pelage. It looks rather like a small, elegant Llama, and is more often seen in open fields, whereas the skulking Muntjac usually favours woodland thickets. These are Bedfordshire's two commonest deer, but my woodland trips this year have also produced sightings of a herd of Fallow Deer, with their diagnostic black-and-white striped rear ends, and a single male Roe Deer, surprised one afternoon as my companion (Judy Knight) and I rounded the edge of a small isolated piece of woodland. We, too, were surprised, and the three of us stared at each other for several moments – moments to be cherished by us.

Unexpected birds have included Crossbills flying across a glade in a conifer wood; a tiny Merlin swishing over bleak farmland; a Goshawk disturbed from its recently killed prey (a Wood Pigeon) at the edge of a woodland ride; Ravens – a new colonist of our county – croaking as they flew overhead; a migrant Wood Warbler, repeatedly singing its shivering trill, evocative of steep Welsh or Scottish valleys; and a magnificent Marsh Harrier watched as it drifted effortlessly across a cloudless sky. Unexpected delights.

Woodland flowers are at their best in spring, when they take advantage of the sunlight penetrating to the woodland floor past leafless branches. Carpets of Bluebells delight both eye and nose, with a sea of colour and sweet perfume, in some places enhanced by the elegant white Wood Anemone and Wood-sorrel. In two marshy spots, we came across patches of Butterbur, its short spikes of purple flowers jutting up from the bare ground long before its huge leaves had developed. Both places were adjacent to churches. Is that a coincidence, or is it significant? Does any reader know whether this strange plant has any religious connections? Perhaps the churches were deliberately built beside a spring associated with earlier, pagan religious ceremonies?

A delightful plant, of which I had heard but which I had never before seen, was discovered by my companion (Judy Knight again) when we were walking along the green lane that is the Icknield Way near Pegsdon. Moschatel is insignificant, growing to only 5-10 centimetres in height, and has equally inconspicuous pale-greenish flowers, with yellow anthers, but look at it closely and it is another little delight. Borne on a short vertical stem, each flowerhead has five little flowers, one pointing directly upwards and the other four pointing sideways, so that the flowerhead looks like a cube, with a flower on each of five sides. This unusual and charming form gives the plant its alternative and very apt name, Townhall Clock.

You never know what you'll find when you go for a walk in the countryside.

First published in *Bedfordshire County Life Magazine* in summer 2004

Natural chiming in the garden

The streets of suburban northern Bedford would not be the first place that one would look for an alien, but they do echo with alien cries every summer evening. Walk or drive around the housing estates at night and you will hear a clear, bell-like "peep" coming unexpectedly from the flower borders, bushy corners or rockeries. The vocalists are Midwife Toads, a species introduced to Britain from Continental Europe in the late nineteenth century, and Bedford is its British headquarters. Smaller than our native Common Toad (which grows up to 12 cm in length) – indeed smaller even than the rarer Natterjack Toad (which may attain 8 cm) – the Midwife Toad is a diminutive 5 cm in length when fully grown.

The Midwife Toad (which has the equally revealing scientific name *Alytes obstetricans*) is so called because the female does not deposit her eggs in a pond as do most other amphibians, but lays them in such a way that the male can twine them around his legs. He then carries them with him for two or three weeks, during their most vulnerable period, finally placing them in a pool of water just as the tadpoles are breaking free.

So far as can be judged, this recently introduced addition to our fauna is benign, posing no major threat to native wildlife (unlike scourges such as the attractive but very destructive American Grey Squirrel and American Mink and the Asiatic Muntjac).

Gardeners and naturalists often have different attitudes to wildlife, although, nowadays, most educated gardeners will regard a few nettles, an elder bush or a bramble patch in a corner of the garden as a welcome 'wildlife haven' rather than as a place harbouring 'pests and vermin'. There are, however, some creatures that have few fans, and the larva of the Solomon's-seal sawfly must surely be high on the list of most-hated garden pests. The grey larvae, which resemble the caterpillars of butterflies and moths, usually appear in June or July and, seemingly in the space of just a couple of days, can reduce the elegant arching shoots of Solomon's seal to bare stems and skeletal leaves. The larvae of a related sawfly can defoliate an entire silver birch tree almost overnight. These insects are, however, more closely related to bees and wasps than to either butterflies and moths or the true flies. When they appear in a garden, it is difficult to view them objectively. Fortunately, however, the plants that they attack seem to be resilient, and survive to provide meals for their insect guests year after year. The grey larvae look somewhat loathsome, and seem to be shunned by birds such as tits that avidly consume caterpillars, so presumably taste unpleasant. Perhaps, like the caterpillars of the Monarch butterfly, they ingest and accumulate poisons from the plant that they eat.

That gardener's friend, the Hedgehog, which loves to eat beetles, slugs and snails, seems to be on the decrease in our county. I have not seen one (or its distinctive blackish droppings filled with insect remains) in my own garden for over a year, and, more worryingly, have seen few squashed corpses on the roads. I deduce not that today's Hedgehogs are better educated and have become more careful when crossing roads (or that today's car-owners drive more slowly or carefully), but that there are fewer Hedgehogs around to be killed. The use of poisonous slug-pellets has been suspected as one cause. So, provided that your garden is a pesticide-free zone, that's where an 'untidy corner' (or mini nature reserve) could help, by providing a safe refuge for a family of

Hedgehogs. With the current fad for decking and paving and gravelled areas to replace lawns and borders, the Hedgehog does need such help.

Road casualties of another mammal have, however, increased noticeably in recent years. Badger corpses by the roadside are now a frequent sight, just as dead Hedgehogs were in the past. Sad as it is to see them, this does suggest that the Badger population is thriving at present, though one has to be very lucky to see one, unless it is caught in the car headlights. Do drive carefully ...

First published in *Bedfordshire County Life Magazine* in autumn 2004

Wildlife Puzzle 12
Q. Blue-eyed Mary, Sweet Cicely, the Gallant Soldier, Sweet Alison, Sweet Violet and Sweet William are all plants that sound like people. Five of the six have something else in common. What is it? A different five have something different in common. What is it? Which are the two odd ones out?

Wildlife Puzzle 13
Q. Apart from the fact that one of them has two words in its name, which of the following is the odd one out? Magpie, Mallow, Mullein, Redshank, Viper's Bugloss

Wildlife Puzzle 14
Q. In what respect are *Saxifraga X urbium* and *Sisymbrium irio* both 'more widespread' than the Furze Wren, the goose that eats eelgrass, the Mourning Cloak or Grand Surprise, and *Dianthus armeria*?

The countryside in winter

On a warm, sunny day in spring or summer, it is easy and natural to think of a trip into the countryside. Resident birds are nesting, there are migrant birds to be discovered, the first Barn Swallows appear and warblers are singing, butterflies and flowers are to be seen along every footpath, Brown Hares cavort in the fields, woodpeckers are drumming from the copses, dragonflies patrol lakes and riversides, and, later, the hedgerows are coloured with berries and other fruits.

Winter is a different matter. It seems natural not to go out in the wind and rain or frost, but to stay in, protected by the central heating. Most trees are leafless, migrant birds have all gone south to warmer climes, bird-song has ceased, crops have been harvested and the fields and woodland seem empty, quiet and lifeless. The impression is that there is little to be seen, and that there is therefore little purpose in braving the inclement elements. What a mistake! There are so many exciting sights and sounds to be experienced by anyone willing to wrap up and venture out into the Bedfordshire countryside in winter. A few memories will serve as examples.

Although some come annually, it is not every year that large numbers of Bramblings cross the North Sea to overwinter in Britain rather than on the Continent. When they do, however, flocks several hundred or even several thousand strong may assemble where food is abundant. This may be with Chaffinches, Yellowhammers and other finches and buntings where grain is scattered in unploughed stubble, near a straw-stack or where horses or Pheasants are fed. More likely, however, they will congregate under beech trees, where the fallen nuts form one of the Brambling's favourite foods. The birds' subtle shades of brown and grey, together with warm orange, in place of a Chaffinch's pink, camouflage the Bramblings wonderfully against the fallen beach leaves, so that it takes time to realise that the one or two seen moving on the woodland floor are actually tens, dozens or hundreds. If they fly, however, their white rumps flash in the gloom of the woodland. To come across such a flock would be a highlight of any winter stroll. Once found, however, they will probably remain, feasting on the beech mast, for weeks, a few sometimes even staying into May, when the males are magnificent, with glossy black heads. The beech hangers along the escarpment from Pegsdon to Barton-le-Clay and west to Sharpenhoe and beyond, or the scattered beech trees in Woburn Park, have in the past provided winter homes for this beautiful northern finch.

Food supply on the Continent (or, rather, the lack of it) affects many species that come to us in larger numbers in some years than in others. Crossbills (usually arriving in July) and Bohemian Waxwings (usually arriving in October-November) are the best-known examples. While the conifer crop and berry crop determine those species' numbers here, the ups and downs of the owl and Kestrel populations are determined by the cyclical variations in numbers of rodents, especially voles and mice. In a 'good' vole year, we are sometimes lucky enough to have Short-eared Owls spending the winter in Bedfordshire, providing a delightful sight at dusk as they quarter areas of rough grassland, such as those at Cardington, Henlow and Thurleigh. Occasionally, a Hen Harrier may linger and join the feast. It is always worth scanning such areas as dusk falls, for even if there is no Short-eared Owl or Hen Harrier, there is still the chance of seeing the ghostly form of a Barn Owl, wavering silently and so easy to miss unless looked for especially. Dusk is often almost as exciting as dawn.

In some years, when severe cold strikes the Continent and their traditional wintering areas in the Low Countries become frozen, a fantastic northern duck may come to Britain in larger than usual numbers. The female and young male Smews are charming enough – small diving ducks with chestnut-coloured crowns and white cheeks, and with serrated mandibles that leads to them (along with the Goosander and the Red-breasted Merganser) being known as sawbills – but the adult males are stunningly beautiful. Once referred to as White Nuns, they are a gleaming white (should we say *Daz*-white?), crossed by a series of sharply defined, thin black lines, a small black mask and a crest that is raised whenever their emotions demand (aggression or courtship). On a snowy day, when a warm hat, scarf and gloves are essential, just one of these little ducks would make the day, and a flock can be an eternal winter memory.

These three examples would be highlights of any winter. We never know, however, what will appear on a winter walk. A slinky Stoat or a Weasel out hunting; a Little Owl mewing from a pollarded willow or an old ash tree; the turquoise flash along the river of a passing Kingfisher; a mixed flock of winter thrushes – Redwings and Fieldfares – feeding on old pasture; the whistles of male Wigeons from the misty distance of a reed-fringed lake on a foggy day. Memories.

First published in *Bedfordshire County Life Magazine* in winter 2004/05

Wildlife gardening for fun?

With spring upon us yet again, we gaze out on cheery snowdrops, glowing daffodils and vivid crocuses. When we venture forth, however, it becomes necessary to assess the work that needs to be done in the winter-ravaged garden.

The wildlife-sensitive gardener will have left most seed-heads in place in the autumn, to provide food for birds and mammals, and hiding places for overwintering invertebrates. Now, however, these need tidying up, weed seedlings need to be hoed, and any beds undug in autumn need to be forked over ready for sowing or planting. Even the smallest plot seems to require a full-time gardener at this busy time of year.

"A wildlife garden is quite different, of course, and needs hardly any work – you can just leave it alone and let the wildlife thrive." I wish!

My own garden has always been managed with wildlife in mind. I have never tidied up unnecessarily, there have always been patches of rough grass, and fallen branches have been left to lie where they fell. I grow some vegetables in an area fenced off to keep the Rabbits out, and flowers and ornamental bushes provide colour in spring, summer and autumn. There is also plenty of flowering and fruiting ivy, but that needs to be kept under control so that trees do not become top-heavy and lose branches or are brought down completely in heavy rain or snowfall.

How much time does one need to devote to a wildlife garden? I estimate that it is probably no less than that needed to maintain an 'ordinary garden'. consisting mainly of lawn and ornamental beds.

Last year, I maintained my usual list of 'things to be

done' in the garden, but, instead of merely crossing them out and throwing the list away when they had been done, I kept a 12-month record of the time devoted to each task. In summary, this was as follows:

Weeding (47 hours)
Trimming and cutting back bushes (39 hours)
Mowing (38 hours)
Cutting back ivy on house and tall trees (18 hours)
Cutting hedges (17 hours)
Spreading manure and compost (16 hours)
Raking leaves (13 hours)
Maintenance (mending fences, etc.) (11 hours)
Clearing debris from small pond (9 hours)
Harvesting fruit & vegetables (7 hours)
Tying up bushes, loganberries, etc. (6 hours)
General tidying (e.g. sweeping patio) (5 hours)
Pruning (4 hours)
Clearing crop remains (runner beans, artichokes, asparagus) (3 hours)
Digging (3 hours)
Watering (2 hours)
Hoeing (1 hour)
Planting or replanting (1 hour)
Pest control (sawfly larvae on Solomon's-seal) (1 hour)
Spreading straw on asparagus and rhubarb beds (1 hour)
Sowing seeds (1 hour)
Dead-heading (1 hour)

The total is 244 hours – less than five hours per week, on average – but I found it revealing that, even in a garden where I welcome many plants that other gardeners might regard as weeds, the most time-consuming job was weeding. Lawn-mowing was formerly a larger task, but is now carried out for me by Rabbits and Muntjacs, so that my lawns are a haze of blue in summer, with the flowers of speedwells, bugle and selfheal. They are springy underfoot, with mossy cushions – so much nicer, in my view, than the coarse grass demanded by gardening experts, and attractive not only to the eye but also to Green Woodpeckers seeking ants.

Are all these garden chores worthwhile? It depends upon

one's priorities, of course, but the pleasure that I get from watching the birds and other animals, discovering interesting plants, and observing the behaviour and interactions of the garden's inhabitants makes it very worthwhile for me. Watching Long-tailed Tits constructing their ball-like nest of feathers in a spiny bush; a Magpie playing 'catch me if you can' with a Red Fox; a Stoat taking a flying leap into the centre of an ornamental pond, swimming around, and then shaking itself like an elongated retriever dog; a Bee-fly hovering stationary and then darting away like a high-powered helicopter; a family party of four newly-fledged Great Spotted Woodpeckers being taught by their parents how not to fall off a branch; groups of inebriated Red Admiral butterflies supping the juice from fallen apples. Those are just a few examples of the fun that a non-manicured plot can provide.

I must end now – there's weeding to be done.

First published in *Bedfordshire County Life Magazine* in spring 2005

Wildlife Puzzle 15

Q. A nice easy one this time: name the two birds, two mammals and three plants hidden in various ways in these three daft sentences:
It is not terribly clever to wear summer lingerie in an Arctic winter. It is, however, if you feel keen to visit a warm spot, and, for example, if Bermuda is your choice for a holiday break. An insect's nip can produce an awful mark, so, if you catch a grasshopper, quickly put it in a box and listen to its chirping.

Wildlife Puzzle 16

Q. Why should a court-martialled Lieutenant-Colonel, a female descendant of a jungle game-bird, and a transitional area between water and land with grassy vegetation but no appreciable peat deposits all remind you of a distinctively shaped entertainment venue?

All change

It has been a good spring for Holly Blues. This small butterfly has pale-blue upper surfaces to its wings and chalky-white under surfaces, with merely a hint of blue, and a scattering of small black dots. Unlike the other blue butterflies, it is found not only in the countryside, but also frequents gardens, even in the centre of towns. It is often seen fluttering vertically up bushes and climbing plants, searching for places to lay its eggs. In spring, the females are seeking Holly bushes, where they lay their eggs near the flower buds. In high summer, however, when a new brood is flying, the females mostly lay their eggs on Ivy. Suburban gardens – especially those that are well-established – usually contain both of these food-plants for the caterpillars.

Unfortunately for the Holly Blue, however, the larvae of a black-and-yellow parasitic wasp (*Listrodomus nychemerus*) feed solely on the caterpillars of the Holly Blue. When the butterfly is abundant, its parasite thrives, so that the number of Holly Blues then crashes, then so too do the numbers of the parasitic wasp. Thus, their populations have high peaks and deep troughs, usually following a six-year or seven-year cycle. This spring, I once had eighteen Holly Blues in sight at once, prospecting Holly bushes in my garden – the most that I have ever seen at one time.

A relatively recent acquisition to my garden is the Speckled Wood, an attractive brown-and-yellow butterfly, mottled to mimic the dappled spots of sunlight on the floor of a wood. The males take up a position on a sunlit leaf and dispute this with any encroaching male in a towering, twisting, fluttering upward flight. The original occupier almost always wins such a dispute, but may lose out if a third male sneaks in to snatch the choice, sunny position while the first two are away on their airborne tussle.

This butterfly has also shown great changes in abundance and distribution in Britain, but on a much longer time-scale. It was probably widespread in the nineteenth century, but its range had contracted and it was confined to the southwest of the United Kingdom in the early years of the twentieth century. It has now expanded back into much of its former range, and is common in Bedfordshire woodland (and natural gardens).

Changes such as these are the norm in nature. Looking at the countryside, the human eye sees a static situation, but every organism from bacteria, fungi and invertebrates to flowering plants, birds and mammals is part of an incredibly intricate, inter-reacting network, also affected by climate, weather and the activities of Man. In reality, almost nothing is static, but is being affected by a multitude of influences.

I have been birdwatching for some 50 years. When I started, I could find nests of Wryneck, Red-backed Shrike and Hawfinch with little effort. Now, none breeds in Bedfordshire. A mere 25 years ago, several pairs of Tree Sparrows and Lesser Redpolls nested in my northeast Bedfordshire garden, but each is now reduced to a handful of pairs in the entire county.

On the other hand, 50 years ago we were mourning the loss of inland colonies of Cormorants from Britain, but they have now come back with a vengeance, thanks to flooded clay-pits and gravel-pits and well-stocked fishing lakes. That elegant little white heron with yellow feet, the Little Egret, was the rarest of all the ten heron-like birds that occurred in Britain. We thought of it as a bird of southern Europe and

Africa that might be seen here just once or twice in a birdwatcher's lifetime, and there were only a dozen British records *ever*. Nowadays, that number is recorded every year in Bedfordshire alone.

Just a couple of decades ago, the Oystercatcher was confined in England to the coast, and occurred very rarely as a migrant in Bedfordshire. Now, it breeds successfully at numerous wetland sites in the county every year, and pairs may even be seen flying over the centre of Bedford itself. Their smart black-and-white plumage, pointed wings, long bright-red bills and loud musical calls make them conspicuous wherever they go.

These are just a few examples. The list of losses is sad, but many lost species may return one day. The additions almost get taken for granted, but in number nearly match the losses. With care, the environment can be improved to welcome colonisers and retain conditions suitable for species under threat. Changes are constantly monitored by the Bedfordshire Natural History Society (www.bnhs.org.uk) and our network of nature reserves is constantly being expanded and managed expertly by the Wildlife Trust for Bedfordshire, Cambridgeshire, Northamptonshire and Peterborough (www.wildlifebcnp.org). If you are interested in helping wildlife locally, these local organisations all deserve your support.

First published in *Bedfordshire County Life Magazine* in summer 2005

Wildlife Puzzle 17

Q. What military connection is there between the tropical, plankton-eating damselfish *Abudefduf saxatilis*, our commonest woodpecker, our second-commonest tit and the Curly Waterweed?

Full of variety

Far from the sea, with no mountains, no fast-flowing rocky-bedded streams or rivers, and less woodland than almost every other county – to an outsider, Bedfordshire might appear to have little to offer the naturalist. There is, however, a huge range of different habitats in our county, with plenty to interest everyone, from the dedicated natural-historian to the casual observer out for a walk alone, with partner, with family, with dog or with all three.

The River Great Ouse and River Ivel meander through their respective valleys with their former floodplains evident but now largely dry, so lacking Snipe, Yellow Wagtails and Redshank, which must have abounded in previous centuries. The Snipe, indeed, is now only a migrant and winter visitor to the county, its spectacular aerial displays and weird 'drumming' (a noise like a bleating sheep, produced by vibrating tail feathers as the bird dives earthwards) are a thing of the past, except on very rare occasions. Yellow Wagtails can still be found, but more usually now in arable fields of potatoes or brassicas than in riverside pasture. Redshanks, however, have taken to the 'new' wetlands that enhance our county: the flooded clay-pits and gravel-pits in the river valleys and farm reservoirs constructed to supply water for crop irrigation. These sites are also the focus for birdwatchers' attention in spring and autumn, when regular migrants such as Swallows, Black Terns, Dunlins and Greenshanks may be joined by rarer birds such as a Garganey, a Temminck's Stint or – as happened this spring – a Great Reed Warbler.

Several of these flooded pits are now maintained as

nature reserves, with public access encouraged. Harrold Country Park, Marston Vale Country Park and Priory County Park in Bedford, for instance, are all popular with both those out for a country stroll and birdwatchers. In winter, they are havens for wildfowl, with a total of 35 species of ducks, geese and swans having been seen, of which more than a dozen occur regularly.

Bedfordshire's greatest natural asset is, however, in my view, the chalk hills that cross the county from Pirton in the east to Whipsnade in the west: Knocking Hoe, Deacon Hill, Pegsdon Hills, Barton Hills, Sharpenhoe Clappers, Sundon Hills, Dunstable Downs and Whipsnade Downs, with outliers such as Totternhoe Knolls. From early spring to late autumn, these areas are renowned to botanists for their specialist flora, with plants such as Pasque Flower, Musk Orchid, Great Pignut and Moon Carrot. Where they are kept short by Rabbits or managed grazing by sheep, the grassland is full of blue Small Scabious, purple Greater Knapweed, yellow Birds'-foot Trefoil and the spikes of Pyramidal Orchids. In high summer, these areas have not only a profusion of flowers, but also high numbers of exciting butterflies, such as Chalkhill Blue, Small Blue, Marbled White and Dark Green Fritillary.

There are many public footpaths, so everyone can enjoy the delights of our county's scenic wonders. Anyone walking in the Deacon Hill or Pegsdon Hills area can then enjoy refreshment at the *Live and Let Live*, conveniently sited at the base of the hills [and, these days, often watch Red Kites overhead at the same time].

First published in *Bedfordshire County Life Magazine* in autumn 2005

Searching and discovering

Every year is different. Winter may follow autumn each year, and in turn become spring, but the changing seasons follow no standard pattern in England. The major weather events – such as the hot summers of 1976 and 2003, the great storm in 1987 and the excessive precipitation and floods of 1947 and 1998 – may linger in our memories, but even the more subtle changes have reverberating effects. Some factor (such as a heavy or late or early frost) may affect an insect which pollinates a certain plant; with smaller numbers of that insect, that plant may set less seed or berries; so the birds or mammals that feed on those fruits may turn to other food; which is therefore less abundant for some other animal; and so on. Thousands, or more probably millions, of such little chains of events mesh with each other to produce startling changes from one year to the next. Unravelling them is the work of ecologists, who study the interactions of plants and animals in the natural environment.

There are rather more species of plants and animals (and fungi and bacteria) than there are ecologists, and the study of any one species (or community of species) takes several years. Only a very few species have ever been thoroughly studied, therefore, and they are mostly those which are of importance (economic importance!) to human beings. Very little is known, compared with what is still to be discovered.

Even in a populous county such as Bedfordshire – with a thriving natural history society, the headquarters of the United Kingdom's major bird conservation organisation (the Royal Society for the Protection of Birds, at Sandy) with its own research department, university campuses at Bedford,

Cranfield and Luton, and museum staff based in Bedford and Luton, together comprising many individual amateur and professional experts – we do not, for many animals and plants, even have a complete list of the species that occur. Biological recording, carried out mostly by thousands of amateur naturalists, co-ordinated by the Biological Records Centre, has accumulated hundreds of thousands of records. These are plotted using the squares of the National Grid, to show the current distributions of plants and animals throughout the United Kingdom. That, however, is only the first stage. How have each of these distributions changed? Are they changing now? If so, why? The answer will be different in almost every case, and each one will, in some way, influence many others.

If this all seems impossibly complicated and daunting, that is not the message that I am trying to impart. The key point is that there is so much still to be learnt, and all of us can – if we wish – make a small contribution to Mankind's knowledge of the natural world. Anyone can, with a little effort, become competent at discovering, identifying and recording a group of plants or animals. How to get started? Join the Bedfordshire Natural History Society and you will instantly have access to other people who will be delighted to share their excitement and their expertise with you.

The weather forecasters are currently predicting that the winter of 2005/06 will be severely cold. If they are right, many animal species will suffer losses, which will in turn affect other animals and plants, sometimes beneficially, sometimes detrimentally. Keeping an eye on such events will help us to understand the network of interactions that make up the living world (or ecosystem, to use modern jargon).

First published in *Bedfordshire County Life Magazine* in winter 2005/06

An important year

Founded in 1946, the Bedfordshire Natural History Society celebrates its Diamond Jubilee this year [2006]. It is being marked in a number of ways, including several special surveys, in which non-members as well as members are being invited to participate.

Where does Mistletoe grow in Bedfordshire? The distinctive ball-shaped clusters of this hemiparasite are especially visible in winter and spring, before they are partly masked by the leaves of their host tree. There is a wonderful set of clumps at Ampthill Park, close to the A418, where there are so many that they are difficult to count, and a large number of clumps is also to be seen in the area around Wrest Park in Silsoe. Where are there others? On which species of host tree are they growing?

How many House Martins nest in Bedfordshire? One of the two single-species bird surveys being run by the Bedfordshire Bird Club this year, as part of the Jubilee celebrations, asks for simple details such as the house number and road name and number of occupied nests. The building of the mud nest is a marvel of construction (the birds even vibrate their bills in the liquid mud to accelerate the hardening process, in just the way that concrete is stimulated mechanically on building sites). Watching the nest-building and then the development and eventual fledging of the nestlings is delightful compensation to home-owners for any mess that may drop onto the pavement below the nest and the chirruping of the nestlings above a bedroom window from soon after dawn.

Another migrant bird that comes to us from Africa every

spring is also being surveyed in the county in 2006. The Swift nests in natural holes in cliffs and old woodpecker holes in trees in some parts of its European range, but in Britain almost all nests are in buildings, often under roof tiles. How many nest in Bedfordshire? Locating all the nests would be an impossible job, so the aim is to count the birds in spring and early summer when screaming parties flash across the skies near their nesting places. Indeed, several of the Swift's old country names reflect these screams and the bird's all-dark plumage: Screecher, Screamer, Jack Squealer, Devil Bird, Deviling, Devil's Screecher, Devil Shrieker, Devil Squealer and Devil's Bitch, for instance. Such vocal groups used to be common in places such as the Market Square at Sandy and around every village church, but are many fewer nowadays. The Swift arrives much later than some other summer migrants, often three or four weeks after the first Swallow, but pairs are usually on their breeding territories by the second week of May.

The BNHS will also be conducting surveys of the very vocal alien Midwife Toads and Glow-worms (which are, of course, actually beetles). They occur in very different places, but both will need special counts at dusk and during the night, when their noises or phosphorescence can be detected. The Midwife Toads of Bedford (and Sharnbrook) were featured just over a year ago [see pages 40-42]. The males carry the fertilized eggs around with them, not depositing them in a pond or puddle until they are just about to hatch. Introduced from the Continent more than a hundred years ago, the Midwife Toad is now well established in many gardens, its "pip" vocalizations sometimes being mistaken for electronic devices.

Glow-worms feed on snails, so are found most frequently

on calcareous soil where snails are especially abundant. They also occur along the old Bedford to Cambridge railway line, doubtless because chalky stones were used in its construction. To see details of surveys like these, visit www.bnhs.org.uk

The year 2006 also sees the start of a massive new survey by the Bedfordshire Bird Club. Back in 1962, the Botanical Society of the British Isles produced the amazing *Atlas of the British Flora*, with the distribution of every plant species shown in maps based on surveys in each of the 3,860-odd 10-km X 10-km squares in Britain and Ireland. This achievement inspired naturalists and biologists to start mapping animals as well as plants, and this has now been carried out in most countries in the World. The botanists produced an even-more-comprehensive *New Atlas of the British and Irish Flora* in 2002, a huge tome, running to over 900 pages. In Bedfordshire, several groups have been mapped using a finer grid, the 2-km X 2-km squares (generally known as tetrads), of which there are 378 in the county. Most notable of these have been John Dony's *Bedfordshire Plant Atlas* published in 1976, and two breeding bird surveys: *Bedfordshire Bird Atlas 1968-77* by B. D. Harding and *An Atlas of the Breeding Birds of Bedfordshire 1988-92* by Rob Dazley & Paul Trodd.

Now, after a gap of 14 years in which birdwatchers have casually noted many changes in bird numbers and distribution, the time has come to repeat this survey. This Bedfordshire survey will coincide with national atlas projects covering the winter as well as the summer in the whole of Britain and Ireland, being co-ordinated by the British Trust for Ornithology and Birdlife Ireland.

It's going to be a busy year for Bedfordshire's naturalists!

First published in *Bedfordshire County Life Magazine* in spring 2006

Swings and roundabouts

After a very dry winter and early spring, the hedgerow trees and bushes were smothered in flowers this year. Seldom can I remember such a show of white blackthorn and pink-and-white hawthorn and apple blossom. This was probably a response to the shortage of water, the plants reacting to possible demise owing to drought by producing an abundance of fruit and seeds. If late spring is relatively frost-free, we may have a bumper berry crop this coming autumn.

It was not the weather here that affected the migrants coming for the summer from the south, but something certainly did. Perhaps drought or perhaps insecticide use in parts of Africa may be among the causes, but certain of our summer migrant birds have been declining fast. There seem to be even fewer Cuckoos cuckooing this summer than there were in 2005 and 2004, and that sound so evocative of warm summer days – the purring of Turtle Doves – is almost a thing of the past. Have you heard any this year? By mid May, I could count the numbers of both these species on the fingers of just one hand, whereas not many years ago they were so numerous that they were taken for granted. The Turtle Doves get shot in southern Europe, but this probably does not contribute significantly to the Cuckoo's decline.

Bird populations rise and fall, often for reasons that we fail to understand. Swings and roundabouts. On the plus side this year, certainly where I have been most in the field, in north Bedfordshire, there have been more Lesser Whitethroats than I can ever remember. Their distinctive rattling song seemed to be coming from every hedgerow, even outnumbering the scratching song of the Common

Whitethroat, and there was no shortage of chiff-chaffing Chiffchaffs or the cascading songs of Willow Warblers. Not all of our migrant birds are in decline.

Some of our resident birds seem to be doing well, too. In the survey of Bedfordshire's woodlands a couple of year ago, members of the Bedfordshire Bird Club discovered that the tiny sparrow-sized Lesser Spotted Woodpecker had declined considerably in numbers, and seemed to be absent from a swathe of woodland along the Greensand Ridge between Everton and Woburn – an area that was formerly its stronghold. The good news is that this year there has been a spate of reports of this delightful bird from sites in the Willington - Moggerhanger - Northill - Old Warden - Southill area. Were they overlooked during the 2004 Woodland Survey, or has there been a rapid increase in numbers, or have they just been particularly active this year? We shall probably never know. This is an elusive species, often quietly feeding among the thin upper branches of tall trees, and seldom seen unless it sings (a rapid "pee-pee-pee-pee-pee…" somewhat similar to the vocalisations of Nuthatch and Kestrel) or drums (rapidly tapping against a resonant dead tree branch). The larger Great Spotted Woodpecker also drums (not to be confused with the tapping made when these birds excavate their nestholes or the opening of hazelnuts and acorns by Great Tits or Nuthatches), but the sequence of taps made by the smaller species is much longer and more uniform, whereas the taps in the short sequence of the larger species run together at the end. Like so many sights and sounds in nature, if you think that it *might be* a Lesser Spotted Woodpecker drumming, it probably isn't, since, if it is, you will *know* that it is.

Now, in high summer, it is the time to make a really

useful contribution to knowledge of Bedfordshire's birds. As noted last month, the county's Natural History Society (and its ornithological wing, the Bedfordshire Bird Club) is carrying out surveys of House Martins and Swifts. Participants have been asked to note the number of House Martin nests (and how many seem to be occupied, with adults visiting or youngsters visible) on each house in their street, and similarly to make a note of any screaming parties of Swifts as they tear around the rooftops (a count of the numbers and the date, plus the locality). [These surveys were co-ordinated for the BBC by Andy Banthorpe.]

Our county has much to offer the nature lover, whether casual enjoyer of aesthetics or serious student of natural history. Enjoyment can be shared in the company of others, either at field meetings (open to all) or lectures, by becoming a member of the Bedfordshire Natural History Society. It is amazing what can be found on a simple country stroll if you are in the presence of experts on butterflies, moths, birds, plants, insects, bats, lichens, fungi and all the other things that make up the natural environment. On a recent visit by members of the Society to the chalk hills at Barton-le-Clay, I was shown the gorgeous Pasque Flowers, the tiny Spring Sedge and the intriguingly named, but hardly beautiful Bloody-nosed Beetle. Inspired by this, I subsequently visited the nearby Pegsdon Hills, where my companion (David Fisher) and I found the wonderfully coloured (and excellently camouflaged) Green Hairstreak butterfly, with its zebra-marked antennae and legs. We celebrated with an *al fresco* lunch at the welcoming *Live and Let Live* pub, nearby at the foot of the hills, watching Common Buzzards circling in the thermals as we dined. Natural history is fun!

First published in *Bedfordshire County Life Magazine* in summer 2006

Desecration!

One of the great natural treasures of Bedfordshire was the wonderful colony of Pasque Flowers on the rounded chalk hillsides at Barton Hills Nature Reserve. Every spring, botanists and nature-lovers from all over the county and beyond would make the pilgrimage to this spot to see the magnificent purple-and-yellow flowers set in all their glory against the green of the short wiry turf. It involved a stiff climb up a steep slope, but was well worth the effort.

Why have the previous sentences been in the past tense? Because, in May this year, someone dug up every one. This was no act of thoughtless vandalism, since it must have involved planning. The perpetrator or perpetrators would have needed a trowel or a spade; boxes to carry away the spoils; and a visit either very early in the morning before even the local dog-walkers were awake or by torchlight under cover of darkness. What did they acquire? Less than one hundred plants, which could have been bought for a matter of a few pounds at a garden centre, and which would have sold for a pittance at a car-boot sale. What did they destroy? Bedfordshire's heritage. A natural wonder. The unique genetic make-up of these particular plants, which had existed on the site for perhaps hundreds or even thousands of years. This selfish and probably thoughtless act was the natural history equivalent of burning a great painting or smashing a stained-glass window in a cathedral.

While botanists and others were depressed by this event, the county's ornithologists were revelling in a purple patch at the gravel-pit site at Broom, where it seemed for a while that every wading bird species on the county's list would appear in the space of a matter of a few days in mid May. There were Dunlins, Turnstones, a Temminck's Stint followed closely by a Little Stint and a Sanderling, Green Sandpiper, Wood Sandpiper, Common Sandpipers, Greenshank, Curlew and Whimbrel, as well as the usual Oystercatchers, Redshanks, Ringed Plovers, Little Ringed Plovers and Lapwings. Added to these were flocks of Black Terns (as well as Common and Arctic Terns), Garganeys, Hobbies and a Marsh Harrier. For a spell, this tiny part of Bedfordshire more closely resembled a marsh on the North Norfolk coast, and birders were out in force with their binoculars, tripods and telescopes, adding to the illusion.

Some summer migrants were in good numbers this year, especially Chiffchaffs, Blackcaps, Common Whitethroats and Lesser Whitethroats, but others continued their downward spiral noted previously. How many cuckooing Cuckoos have you heard this year? How many purring Turtle Doves? Not many would be my guess. At one time, both were so common in Bedfordshire that we took them for granted. Now, a cuckooing male Cuckoo is a notable event (though one did stay around my home in Blunham, cuckooing throughout June), and a bubbling female Cuckoo seems to be an even rarer sound. There are also very few places now where the peaceful purring of a Turtle Dove can be heard on a sultry summer afternoon, yet I can remember the time when my companion (James Ferguson-Lees) and I found fourteen Turtle Dove nests in a single hedgerow. The decline of Spotted Flycatchers in eastern England (but apparently not in western Britain) is currently being investigated by the Royal Society for the Protection of Birds. A nest in my garden is currently being monitored by a remotely controlled camera installed by the RSPB's research team, recording every visit by the adults and is poised to detect any predator that may visit the nest.

Walking along the River Ivel and the River Ouse this summer, the repetitive song of Reed Warblers was commoner than the erratic scratchy song of Sedge Warblers, yet the latter generally outnumber the former by five or even ten to one. Were Reed Warblers especially common this year? Perhaps. But Sedge Warblers were certainly much scarcer than usual in the Blunham-Tempsford-Great Barford area. Was this just a local decrease, or part of a national decline? After the end of the breeding season, the British Trust for Ornithology will be able to tell us. In addition to the Trust's professional team, amateur birdwatchers contribute 1.5 million hours of counting each year, in censuses and surveys designed to detect the changing levels of bird populations. The information is used by conservationists and by government, at both national and international levels, and would be impossibly expensive without the time given freely by thousands of willing volunteers. They wear their haloes when they slide reluctantly out of bed before dawn to carry out the work which is later collated, analysed and summarised by the BTO staff. Little wonder that such dedicated birdwatchers cringe when they are referred to as twitchers (a term which should be reserved to describe someone who travels to watch a bird that has already been found and identified by someone else, regarded by some people as the ornithological equivalent of train-spotting, since it contributes nothing to scientific knowledge). Even the most dedicated ornithologist does, however, become a twitcher on occasions, such as when a Snowy Owl appears or a flock (known as a trip) of summer-plumaged Dotterels turns up on migration.

Every country walk can provide interesting surprises,

whether it is a distant view of the landscape, a historical relic or an interesting animal or plant. Although there are some excellent identification guides, I always find, when I consult a book on returning home, that the dragonflies and damselflies that seemed so distinctive when I saw them have some very similar species with which they could be confused. This year, however, when strolling along the banks of the River Great Ouse, I saw several large ginger-brown dragonflies that I knew I had never seen before. It was such a distinctive species, with golden wings and orange-and-black body, that I identified it easily as a Scarce Chaser *Libellula fulva.* I was delighted to find that not only was it indeed scarce in Britain (found in only half a dozen isolated pockets in southern England), but it was also scarce in Bedfordshire, having first been observed only as recently as July 1998. Since then, it has spread along the River Great Ouse, to the site where I saw it and beyond. This is all documented in a very impressive and wonderfully illustrated book, *Dragonflies of Bedfordshire*, by Steve Cham (published by the Bedfordshire Natural History Society, ISBN 0 9506521 7 2).

Another rare dragonfly – the Red-veined Darter *Sympetrum fonscolombii* – provided excitement in the county this summer, and it was also a great year for butterflies, with Silver-washed Fritillaries *Argynnis paphia* appearing in half-a-dozen or more woods where they had not been seen for decades, almost every garden will have been visited by beautiful Painted Ladies *Vanessa cardui* and Red Admirals *V. atalanta*, and the spectacular Hummingbird Hawk-moths *Macroglossum stellatarum* and migrant Silver Ys *Autographa gamma* were widespread. Not all natural history news is doom, gloom and despondency.

First published in *Bedfordshire County Life Magazine* in autumn 2006

Migration

Some of the greatest natural spectacles are provided by migration. Via television, we have all seen the vast herds of Wildebeests crossing the African plains in search of seasonal grazing and enduring the predation of Crocodiles during river crossings. We all know nowadays that a Swallow that nests in an outbuilding in Britain will spend the winter in South Africa and then find its way back to the very same outbuilding in the following summer. By the use of individual marking with small numbered metal rings on the birds' legs, we also now know that a Pied Flycatcher will spend successive winters in the same Acacia tree in Africa as well as returning to the same nest-box in a Welsh oakwood. Amazing!

Most bird migration occurs at night, for the birds need to spend the daylight hours feeding, to accumulate the fat reserves needed to supply the energy for sustained flight. The exceptions to this rule are provided by birds – such as the Swallow – that can feed while they are migrating, or which travel great distances not by flying, but by gliding – such as the hawks, eagles and storks, which utilise thermals to gain height without much energy expenditure and then travel huge distances on a shallow downwards glide to the next thermal.

Despite these generalisations, it is possible to observe some migration in progress during the day, even in an inland county such as Bedfordshire. During daylight, birds often follow geographical features, such as river valleys or lines of hills (and even, on some occasions, man-made features, such as motorways). During the main migratory seasons of March to May and August to October, the birdwatchers who visit

Priory Park in Bedford often observe migrating parties of birds travelling west or east along the valley of the Great Ouse. The line of low hills from Hitchin to Upper Sundon similarly provides a guiding line for migrants. This autumn, flocks of 'winter thrushes' (Redwings and Fieldfares) from Scandinavia, Finland and Russia have provided me with some exciting days from a vantage point on those hills at Sharpenhoe Clappers, and other observers on the Pinnacle above Sandy have seen an even larger passage of these autumn migrants. Spectacular though these movements may be, they represent only a tiny fraction of the mass movements that are going on, unseen, mostly at night, over the whole of the Northern Hemisphere, as millions of birds vacate the cold and relatively foodless northern latitudes for the food-rich south each autumn. The winter thrushes will be feeding on our berry crop; the Swallows and flycatchers will be feasting on African flies. To see the full scale of this mass movement, of which Britain sees only the fringe, one needs to make a visit to one of the Continental focal points, such as the tiny German island of Heligoland in the German Bight or one of the cols in the Alps, where bird migration can be as spectacular as that of those Wildebeest herds.

First published in *Bedfordshire County Life Magazine* in winter 2006/07

Wildlife Puzzle 18
Q. What is the connection between Avocet *Recurvirostra avosetta*, Badger *Meles meles*, Hobby *Falco subbuteo* and Muntjac *Muntiacus reevesi*?

Wildlife Puzzle 19
Q. Which is the odd one out: Baneberry, Cob-nut, Gladdon, King-cup or Ling?

Messengers of spring

The news on radio, television and the daily papers is full these days of examples of the effects of climate change and global warming. We have probably all noticed the unseasonable flowering of many garden plants, and a short walk in mid-Bedfordshire countryside on Christmas Eve revealed 37 wild plants in flower when there might have been only half-a-dozen in a 'normal' year.

Ever since the mid 1940s, members of the Bedfordshire Natural History Society and the Bedfordshire Bird Club have noted the arrival and departure of summer and winter migrants, noting the 'first dates' and 'last dates' for each species. These have recently been collated by Rob Dazley, and analysis of the arrival dates for 19 'typical migrants' (e.g. Cuckoo, Swallow, House Martin, Sedge Warbler, Willow Warbler and Chiffchaff) reveals a striking and consistent pattern.

Compared with arrivals during the 24 years 1946-69, these migrants arrived on average 4 days earlier during the 25 years 1970-94. Only two of the 19 species arrived later in the second period, in each case by just one day, the 17 others all arriving earlier. In the most recent 11-year period, from 1995 to 2005, these same 19 migrants arrived on average 6 days earlier than during the previous period (not a single species arriving later), and, thus, a massive 10 days earlier than during 1946-69. To give just one specific example for a familiar species: House Martins arrived on average on 11th April in the mid 1940s-1960s, on 8th April in the 1970s to mid 1990s, and on 2nd April in recent years. This earlier arrival is accelerating. It is not as dramatic or worrying as the melting of the polar ice-caps, but the ordinary observations of ordinary Bedfordshire birdwatchers have provided another small piece of evidence. Even some of the most reluctant of the world's political leaders now acknowledge the fact of global climate change and the urgent need to take drastic action.

Now is the time to be looking for those spring migrant birds, just arriving back after overwintering in Africa. Expect to see the first **Sand Martins** and **Swallows** in mid March, to see the first **House Martins** and hear the first **Willow Warblers** in early April, to hear the first **Cuckoos** and **Nightingales** in mid April, and to see the first **Spotted Flycatchers** returning to churchyards and favoured gardens in early May.

The observations of Bedfordshire's birds are summarised every year in *The Bedfordshire Bird Report*, published as part of *The Bedfordshire Naturalist* by the BNHS. For details, visit www.bedsbirdclub.org.uk or www.bnhs.org.uk

First published in *Bedfordshire County Life Magazine* in spring 2007

Wildlife Puzzle 20
Q. Combine these 18 three-letter groups to make a plant and four animals:
CHA REL WER LDF RCE SCA FIE QUE ILE SER ARE
PAS GRE CRO UIR COD YSQ COD FLO

Wildlife Puzzle 21
Q. Of these seven birds, which is the odd one out, and why? Common Shelduck, Manx Shearwater, Upcher's Warbler, Crab-plover, Northern Wheatear, Atlantic Puffin and Common Kingfisher

Observations

Watching wildlife requires a whole range of equipment. Bug-hunters carry a net, a range of different-sized glass or plastic jars and a hand lens to examine the minutiae of anatomical structures. Botanists also carry a hand lens, whereas butterfly-watchers need close-focusing binoculars as well as a net. Bat experts are likely to carry high-tech electronic equipment. Birdwatchers certainly need binoculars, and these days most also carry a telescope mounted on a tripod for instant distant viewing. Everyone seems to carry a digital camera.

The various groups of animals and plants also require differing techniques. Mammal-watchers need to cultivate patience, and the ability to remain silent and motionless for long periods. These are also useful attributes for birdwatchers, though many do not take full advantage. Sitting or standing silently beside a clump of bushes or a reedbed will often reveal birds of which the would-be observer walking past is totally oblivious. The secret, of course, is for the wild animals to be unaware that there is a human being nearby. For this reason, most naturalists choose to wear dull clothing that will merge with the surrounding habitat. A few birders (as modern birdwatchers tend to call themselves) deliberately wear red or brightly coloured shirts or coats, apparently taking a 'macho' stance to demonstrate that they can find birds despite being conspicuous. Rather more wear bright colours through ignorance (club outings tend always to include a few such). Most birdwatchers, however, are aware that it is better to be dressed quietly as well as to behave quietly.

Whilst glowing red and fluorescent orange may be

recommended for survival clothing – easy for a rescuer to spot – and most European birdwatchers opt for khaki, greens and browns (unless planning to visit a 'sensitive' military area), it is less well appreciated that white is as bad as red. Indeed, in woodland or forest, red is far better than white (except in those conditions of distant memory, midwinter snows). Even in some open areas, such as moorland, gleaming white stands out where even the *verboten* red can merge with the surroundings.

So, check through those tee-shirts. You may find that you get better or longer views of mammals and birds if they do not realise that you are there watching them.

Some birders find more rare and unusual birds than do others who spend just as much time 'in the field'. Why? It's not *necessarily* that they are 'better birders' or more competent at bird identification. The major secrets are care and perseverance.

It is so tempting to arrive at a favourite site – let's say a local flooded gravel-pit on a June morning – and scan through the swimming wildfowl to pick out the hoped-for rarity – a Black-necked Grebe or a Garganey, perhaps – amongst the Great Crested Grebes, Tufted Ducks and Mallards. Nothing worth seeing? "Right, let's go on to a second site." Tempting, but to be avoided.

With a little self control and discipline, try looking at every single individual duck and grebe. Indeed, identify *every* bird (and age and sex it if you can). That's the way that the 'better birder' finds more rarities – not just the glorious male Garganey, but also the nondescript sleeping female Blue-winged Teal. Scanning a flock and picking out the one that 'looks a bit odd' is lazy birding. Careful perusal of every bird will repay your efforts time and again. (And while you are about it, make counts and send in your records to your county bird recorder, who will always welcome receiving your information.)

This principle applies not just to flocks of wildfowl. It is so easy to say to yourself, as a 'Little Brown Job' disappears into the undergrowth, "Oh, it was probably only a Robin". The observer who checks out every such bird (within reason) is the person who will find the Bluethroat or the Barred Warbler.

It is the same with that distant speck on a telegraph wire. It's easy to say or think "It's probably only a Mistle Thrush" and to walk on. Don't be lazy! Look through your binoculars or telescope. It may often turn out that it is indeed a Mistle Thrush, but sometimes it will be a Kestrel or a Cuckoo or a Turtle Dove, occasionally it may be a rare midsummer Fieldfare, and there's always the faint chance that it may be a Red-footed Falcon or even a Roller. It is worth checking every bird that you see.

Do you know bird songs and calls? If not, by far the best way of learning them is to hear the sound and then to track each one down to its source. That way, you are likely to remember the sound the next time that you hear it. Beware, however, the hidden Chaffinch singing in the same tree as the conspicuously perching silent Yellowhammer (or vice versa)!

First published in *Bedfordshire County Life Magazine* in summer 2007

Wildlife Puzzle 22
Q. Four questions: (1) Which animal went around? (2) Which animal is found on board? (3) Which animal would be welcome in the Ku-Klux Klan? (4) Which plant is a Bedfordshire village?

Spreading or contracting?

This summer has been a busy season for members of the Bedfordshire Bird Club and Bedfordshire Natural History Society, as well as other birdwatchers in the county. Fieldwork for the third Breeding Bird Atlas of Bedfordshire was launched in March, following on those covering 1968-77 and 1988-92. The aims are to show the distribution of breeding birds in the county, using as recording units the 2-km x 2-km squares ('tetrads') of the National Grid (of which there are 378 in the county). Within each of these, an attempt is made to find every bird species and to confirm breeding, using standard evidence. It is usually not necessary to try to find nests, since adult birds carrying food for their nestlings or recently fledged young birds or adults entering or leaving a nest or nest-hole are all equally good evidence of breeding.

This time around, the aim is to cover the whole of the county in six years (2007-11), the last five of which coincide with the third National breeding bird atlas project, run by the British Trust for Ornithology, the Scottish Ornithologists' Club and BirdWatch Ireland.

After just one of the six years, and with many results still to come in, it is already clear that there have been remarkable changes in the 15 years since the second survey. Some species (such as Lesser Redpoll and Turtle Dove) have declined in numbers and contracted their ranges, and some have become extinct in the county (e.g. Hawfinch and Willow Tit), whereas others have increased and expanded their ranges (e.g. Hobby and Oystercatcher). Apart from these dramatic changes, the careful fieldwork and precise mapping method will doubtless show up other less obvious changes. I feel very fortunate to have participated in all three surveys, and I am impatiently awaiting the opportunity to see the final maps when they are produced in 2012.

Meanwhile, I have been enjoying the fieldwork. It is enormously satisfying to think that every observation, even of something as mundane as a Song Thrush carrying a billful of worms to a hidden nest or a Moorhen with a brood of downy youngsters, has value in the documentation of present-day distributions. In late June, noisy young woodpeckers loudly advertise the locations of their nest-holes, and by early July noisy nestling Kestrels, Sparrowhawks and Common Buzzards are doing the same, to the distress of their anxious parents, which try to lure human beings (and other potential predators) away by chattering, swooping and making themselves even more obvious. It is also very satisfying to suspect that a species ought to be present in an area, to seek out the appropriate habitat and then find that the bird is indeed there – a Corn Bunting singing its jangling song on some set-aside, Yellow Wagtails feeding nestlings in a potato field or Little Owls sitting in an old pollarded willow.

Who knows what will come or go in the next few decades? In the first Bedfordshire Atlas, which ended a mere 30 years ago, Willow Tits were found in 29% of the county's tetrads, yet now there is none. Back then, a few Common Buzzards were seen in summer, but none was breeding, yet now this may be the county's commonest raptor, perhaps exceeding in numbers both Kestrel and Sparrowhawk. Thirty years ago, nobody predicted that Willow Tits would go, or that Common Buzzards would recolonise the county. At present, it seems that Bullfinches, Linnets and House Sparrows are all in decline, but will they continue to diminish in numbers or make a comeback?

To learn more, consult *Bedfordshire Bird Atlas* by B. D. Harding (1979) and *An Atlas of the Breeding Birds of Bedfordshire* 1988-92 by R. A. Dazley & P. Trodd (1994), both published by the Bedfordshire Natural History Society (ISBN 0950652105 and 0950652148).

Are House Martins nesting under the eaves of your or a neighbour's house? Are there Swifts nesting in your local church tower? Have you seen Kingfishers entering their bankside nest-tunnel? Have you seen Tawny Owls with fluffy fledglings or a Barn Owl hunting this summer? If you can provide details of the exact date and location (preferably a map reference), the Bedfordshire Bird Club would like to know (visit www.bnhs.org.uk).

First published in *Bedfordshire County Life Magazine* in autumn 2007

Wildlife Puzzle 23
Q. What do the missing parts of the English names of these plants have in common?
(1) _ _ _ dew, (2) _ _ _ _ wort, (3) _ _ _ _ _ nut (also known as Pignut), (4) _ _ _ _ _ 's-looking-glass and (5) Dog's- _ _ _ _ _ _ _

Wildlife Puzzle 24
Q. Where do their names suggest that you might you find the following, and which one is the lowliest? A flightless bird, the second-largest in its family, that builds no nest; the Wild Arum; Europe's only Metalmark; a moth in the family Lithosiinae with long narrow forewings that cloak the body like a stiff Victorian coat; the Milkweed butterfly; and a common and widespread European fritillary that breeds only rarely in Britain.

Taking the high ground

The season that has just passed saw small groups of Bedfordshire's birdwatchers forcing themselves to crawl out of bed in the early hours and leave home while it was still dark, to position themselves on prominent hilltops by dawn. Why? To observe and count the autumn migration of birds through the county. On most days, just a few passing migrants were counted, but on a handful of occasions there were some spectacular movements, with Chaffinches, Bramblings, Redwings, Fieldfares and Wood Pigeons streaming past. Observation points on the Greensand Ridge included The Pinnacle at Sandy, perhaps one of the best sites in Bedfordshire, first investigated last year by Steve Blain from the RSPB, and other vantage points included Deacon Hill, Sharpenhoe Clappers and Sundon Park on the northern escarpment of the Chiltern ridge extending from Hitchin in Hertfordshire to Dunstable.

These observations of visible migration (colloquially referred to these days as "vis mig") do, of course, represent only a tiny proportion of the huge movements that occur unseen overhead, as shown by radar. Much of the migration takes place at night and above the clouds, too high to be observed from the ground even if there were no clouds. At some places, however, and in the right conditions (right for the birdwatchers, but decidedly wrong for the birds!), the numbers involved can be apparent on the ground. This autumn, for instance, some 270,000 Chaffinches were observed at Falsterbo in southern Sweden, and on another day about 36,000 Redwings were grounded upon the tiny German island of Heligoland. These are numbers of which

Bedfordshire observers can only dream, but even in the high hundreds or low thousands, the passage of migrating birds passing in a steady stream southwards or westwards across our county can provide an exciting sight.

Amongst the flocks of common migrants, there are occasionally a few rarer birds, and these, too, can enliven a dawn watch. Some species are unexpected migrants – Great Spotted Woodpeckers, for instance, which we usually think of as resident in our local woodlands – appearing as dots in the distance, passing overhead and then continuing until mere dots in the opposite direction. Inevitably, there are also birds that evade identification. Sometimes (perhaps usually) these will be common birds seen insufficiently well to enable a correct identification to be made, but on other occasions they will provide a real mystery. There have been a few this autumn – a bunting with a call like a Chiffchaff was one, flying past and utterly foxing its bemused observer. Such birds are termed "hoodwinks", an epithet popularised in the 1950s by Professor Maury Meiklejohn. One bird that appeared this autumn over Sharpenhoe Clappers might have been a hoodwink, but did get at least partially identified. Its loud, hoarse squawk attracted attention as it appeared overhead, and the observer was amazed to see a huge, long-tailed bird the size of a Pheasant flying towards Barton-le-Clay. Clearly, someone, somewhere, had lost a Macaw from his or her aviary. You never know what you are going to see when you are birdwatching, even in Bedfordshire.

Indeed, it's not just birds that create exciting wildlife moments, and they can be when one least expects them. Leaving the fully-booked *Hare & Hounds* in Old Warden in search of another restaurant with an available table for dinner, our car headlights lit up a Stoat-like mammal at the side of the road. It did not run away, but stood looking at us as we passed. Its rounded face, rounded ears, humped rear-end and diagnostically bandit-like black-on-pale facemask revealed it to be a Polecat. Not many years ago, Polecats were to be found only in Wales, but – like Common Buzzards and Ravens – have spread eastwards and have now reached Bedfordshire. Most – like Badgers – are seen only as road-kill corpses, so my companion (Nicky Phalasuk) and I counted ourselves as very fortunate to get such a good view of this exciting, shy predator. It provided the subject for mealtime conversation when we reached an alternative restaurant in Sandy.

First published in *Bedfordshire County Life Magazine* in winter 2007/08

Wildlife Puzzle 25
Q. Burrow, Drey, Earth, Form, Holt and Lodge. Beaver, Fox, Hare, Otter, Rabbit, Squirrel and Stoat. Which of the mammals has been given nowhere to live?

Wildlife Puzzle 26
Q. What do the following have in common: (1) a marsh bird with a display flight in which it sounds like a galloping horseman, (2) the old country name for the yellow-flowered wild relation of Salsify, now known as Goat's-beard, and (3) a crow with a black 'face', white eyes and a grey neck?

Wildlife Puzzle 27
Q. Who or what do the following have in common: (1) the Common Swift *Apus apus*, (2) the Small Manta *Mobula hypostoma*, (3) the Orange Hawkweed *Hieracium aurantiacum*, (4) the Widemouth Blindcat, a cave-dwelling catfish, and (5) the foodplant of the caterpillars of the Marsh Fritillary?

Busy counting

There are now three bird-atlas mapping projects being undertaken in Bedfordshire. The Bedfordshire Bird Club started its third scheme to map the county's breeding birds last summer. This winter, the British Trust for Ornithology (together with the Scottish Ornithologists' Club and BirdWatch Ireland) launched schemes to map the distribution and numbers of birds throughout Britain and Ireland in the winter as well as in the summer.

Thus, Bedfordshire birdwatchers who enjoy contributing to county and national research projects will be busy doing so for the next four years. The methods are very simple. It is necessary merely to visit 2-km × 2-km squares (known as tetrads) of the National Grid (these are blocks of four of the 1-km × 1-km squares that are shown on every Ordnance Survey map) and make a note of every bird that is seen or heard. For the BTO surveys, observers concentrate on recording and counting for one or two precisely timed hours in two periods of the winter or summer, whereas for the Bedfordshire survey the emphasis is on finding every species in each tetrad, so longer visits are required, but not counts. Information gathered for the BTO's summer project will be of value for the Bedfordshire scheme, and Bedfordshire Bird Club data will be useful to supplement the BTO's counts. Although this may sound complicated, it isn't. Let me now take you on an actual survey walk that I made in the Blunham area (tetrad TL15K) on 6th January this year.

Setting off along the Kingfisher Way, starting at The Trap – the weir upstream of Blunham Church – there was a singing Dunnock and a singing Robin, with Blue Tits in the white poplar and Chaffinches feeding beside the footpath. Some Wood Pigeons crashed noisily through branches of the alders beside the river and I could hear the chattering of a Magpie and the "teacher" song of a Great Tit. A Great Spotted Woodpecker gave away its position in an ash tree by its hard "chick" call-note and a Green Woodpecker was yaffling simultaneously. There were several Long-tailed Tits along with more Blue and Great Tits and a charm of Goldfinches in the alders. A Moorhen called, and then I spotted several Siskins feeding with the Goldfinch flock. A total of 13 species had been found in the first five minutes, all before passing through the second kissing-gate.

The open horse-pasture had several feeding Blackbirds and single Mistle Thrush and Fieldfare, but I then found no new species until I had passed through the tunnel under the old Bedford-to-Cambridge railway-line, which is now the Sandy-to-Bedford cycle-path. The bushes on the old railway embankment held a pair of Bullfinches uttering their weak but distinctive squeaky calls, there were a couple of Pied Wagtails around the Abbey Corrugated industrial site, and the first Wren of the day rattled from a hedge-bottom.

After crossing the River Ivel by the Bailey bridge, the private fishing area of Kingfisher Lakes can be viewed from the public footpath when leaning on an old iron gate. Wildfowl there included Mute Swans, a Cormorant, small numbers of Tufted Ducks, Gadwalls, Mallards and Coots, together with a Grey Heron and a single Black-headed Gull. The best bird of the day then revealed its presence: the clicking calls and unnerving screams of a Water Rail, which unfortunately – but typically – remained hidden in the reed-beds. Low, musical calls coming from the opposite side of the Ivel revealed the presence of a small spring of Teal on the

South Mills lakes. As the first hour of counting came to an end, at the extreme south-eastern corner of TL15K, a single Song Thrush, two raucous Jays and a flock of 25 Redwings brought the total to 225 birds of 32 species.

After returning to my starting point at The Trap, I then walked downstream along the Ivel, where the Kingfisher Way follows the eastern bank of the river. A Goldcrest called shrilly from an ivy-covered bush, and the tinkling calls and bouncing flight of 16 Goldfinches feeding on the seeds of teasels and burdocks reminded me, as always, of their old country name, 'Lady with the Twelve Flounces.' The arable fields between Blunham and Sandy held feral flocks of 97 Greylag Geese and 36 Canada Geese, all the progeny of stock introduced years ago for sport and ornament, but now grazing like hordes of rabbits on the growing crops. A flock of pigeons turned out to be elegant Stock Doves, not the much more numerous, lumpy Wood Pigeons.

In winter, when the trees are leafless, good views can be had from the Kingfisher Way of the birds on Blunham Lake. On this day, the wildfowl included Wigeon, Pochard and Goldeneye, while the trees on the lake's island held not only 16 Cormorants, but also a single Little Egret, that all-white heron that is rapidly colonising Britain and Ireland. Disappointingly, this stretch of the river did not have the expected Kingfisher or Grey Wagtail, but a hovering Kestrel was hunting over the fields and there was a flock of six Little Grebes on the next lake, near Blunham's Twin Bridges.

Entering the northeastern end of the village, chattering House Sparrows, wheezing Collared Doves and a single Starling on the rooftops were all new for the day. A final stroll up The Drift towards the open agricultural fields between Blunham and Great Barford revealed some unploughed stubble. Wonderful! This was a common winter habitat once, when spring ploughing was the norm, but is much rarer now than it was in the mid twentieth century. Its value as a source of winter food for finches, buntings and game-birds was soon revealed by a huge flock of Yellowhammers, the males' brilliant plumage gleaming in the afternoon sunshine. I counted 80, and there could have been more. Disappointingly, I detected no Sky Lark, but three Meadow Pipits in the same area were the final species as my second hour of counting came to an end in the far northwestern corner of TL15K.

The second hour had produced 533 birds of 42 species (more than in the first hour), and the total for this short two-hour walk was 758 individuals of 47 species. Easy – and fun – to do. Anyone with knowledge of our common British birds could take part and assist in the collection of the information for the next *Atlas of the Birds of Britain and Ireland*. [Bedfordshire's BTO Representative, Nigel Willets, co-ordinated this survey.] Even casual sightings of the scarcer species (e.g. Grey Partridge, Woodcock, Barn Owl, Little Owl, Kingfisher) are valuable contributions, and details with the date and the exact site will still be welcomed by the Bedfordshire Bird Club (see www.bedsbirdclub.org.uk).

First published in *Bedfordshire County Life Magazine* in spring 2008

Wildlife Puzzle 28
Q At the table, place in decreasing value (a) 75% of maples and Sycamore, (b) the bird renowned for nesting down chimney pots, (c) the ancient horseshoe crab, and (d) a butterfly that is widespread on the Continent, but occurs rarely in Britain, though it established a colony in Suffolk briefly in the 1990s.

Then and now

Times change. When I started birdwatching, in Kent, back in the mid 1950s, it was three months before I met another birdwatcher, although I was frequenting several renowned sites for seeing birds. He took me under his wing (sorry for the pun!), and I learned a great deal from him. A veteran of the trenches in the First World War, he was stone-deaf as a result of the gunfire, so I was his ears, which may be why I still rely greatly on the songs and calls that I hear. He, however, amazed me by identifying a flock of Teal at a range of half a mile and distinguishing Wood Sandpipers from Green Sandpipers in flight. His name was W. G. Jarvis. I never discovered what the W or the G stood for, and I always addressed him as "WGJ." As well as teaching me about the birds, he showed me wonderful birdwatching sites, including many on the North Kent marshes. It was only on very rare occasions that we spotted anyone else on the sea-walls. Every bird that we saw was our own discovery.

Nowadays, news of rare and unusual birds arrives almost instantaneously, via mobile phones, text messaging and the internet. Within minutes, twitchers can be heading towards the site of the latest rare-bird sighting.

It was not always so. In April 1961, when I lived in Southampton, I received a postcard telling me the exciting news that a Sociable Plover had been found near Wimborne in Dorset. After waiting impatiently for the weekend, I travelled to search for this Asiatic rarity, but failed to find it. I later discovered that it had last been seen more than a week earlier. Perhaps it was this experience that has made me avoid twitching in the subsequent half century.

Back in those days, of course, the word 'twitching' had only just been coined. People who were interested in seeing rare birds were generally referred to as 'listers' or 'tickers', since they usually maintained a 'life list' and literally ticked off each new bird as they saw it. In those days, when many people did not own a car and there was no motorway network to facilitate speedy travel around the country, chasing after rare birds was a minority activity. Nowadays, hundreds of twitchers may congregate at the location of a single major rarity, and almost all birdwatchers twitch (yes, it is used as a verb as well as a noun!) every now and again.

What is the difference between an ornithologist, a birdwatcher, a birder and a twitcher? Essentially, the general term is birdwatcher, and that covers everyone who looks at birds for pleasure. An ornithologist is someone who undertakes scientific study of birds; he or she will usually, but not necessarily, be a birdwatcher. The term birder originated in North America, where it was synonymous with the European birdwatcher, but here has become less general, referring now to those birdwatchers who specialise in and become skilled at identifying birds. The twitcher is a birder who is willing to travel considerable distances to see a rare bird that has already been found and identified by someone else. In the media, the word twitcher is often misused to describe someone who is actually a birder. Bill Oddie, for instance, constantly suffers from this; he may occasionally twitch, but he is essentially a respected and highly skilled birder.

Twitchers may be looked down upon by those birders who consider that they are the ornithological equivalent of train-spotters, but the ways in which individual human beings gain pleasure from watching birds are, surely, all equally valid?

The poet or the artist – and many 'ordinary birdwatchers' – delight in the sheer beauty of the birds' plumage or behaviour, the birder gets pleasure from finding and identifying scarce birds, and ornithologists gain satisfaction from providing data which may be useful in understanding more about avian biology or be helpful for conservation.

The derivation of the term twitcher is a fascinating story. Back in the 1960s, four friends often went birdwatching together on a *Lambretta* and a *Matchless*. The couple on the *Lambretta* were accompanied by their dog, which they wedged between them. On a cold winter's day, therefore, they arrived at the destination warm, in contrast to the pillion passenger on the *Matchless*, who arrived shivering with cold. They regularly made fun of him, mimicking his twitchings as he shivered and attempted to light his cigarette, and referred to their outings to see rare birds as 'going on a twitch.' Those so involved then, naturally, became known as twitchers. The owner of the *Matchless*, Bob Emmett, wrote about this in 1983 in the journal *British Birds* (volume 76, pages 353-354). His pillion passenger was Howard Medhurst, who can, therefore, be identified as the original twitcher – though he would certainly prefer to be regarded as a birder. Not many words in the English language have such a clearly defined and somewhat humorous conception.

Nowadays, some twitchers have literally gone from one end of the United Kingdom to the other in response to the news of a rare bird, travelling by helicopter, car, 'plane and boat from the Isles of Scilly, west of Land's End, to Shetland, north of John o'Groats, in an attempt to see a single vagrant bird from Siberia – a far cry from my abortive attempt to see a long-gone plover in Dorset.

First published in *Bedfordshire County Life Magazine* in summer 2008

A walk on the wild side

Whereas the impression given to the general public is that birdwatchers are obsessed with rare birds, that is but one small part of the spectrum of interests of ordinary birdwatchers. What constitutes a 'good day' will depend upon each person's individual inclination, but there are certain sights and sounds that excite almost everyone. The spectacle of a Peregrine Falcon hunting, the skill of an Osprey fishing, or the flashy beauty of a pair of displaying Kingfishers create images which may remain as vivid memories years after the sighting itself. These are not everyday events, but, nevertheless, can – with luck – all be seen in our county.

We do make our own luck. The 'lucky' people who see exciting wildlife spectacles are generally those who 'put in the time'. The more often that you take a country walk, the more likely you are to see, say, a hunting Stoat or a gaudy red-and-white Fly Agaric toadstool. Indeed. It will be only rarely that – if you keep your eyes and ears alert to what is around you – you will take a country stroll and not see or hear something interesting, exciting or beautiful. Take a good look at a pair of Bullfinches, the male with his bright red breast and belly contrasting with his glossy black crown and gleaming white undertail-coverts and rump, and his mate with her more subdued but subtly beautiful soft-brown underparts. Their quiet, piping calls are distinctive, but easily overlooked. Bullfinches are widespread in our countryside, favouring overgrown hedgerows, but just sufficiently scarce to make a sighting noteworthy.

At this time of year, hirundines (Swallows, House Martins and Sand Martins) are congregating prior to their departure for their wintering grounds in Africa. Scores or even hundreds may collect on telegraph wires during the day, often sweeping off, as if preparing for but hesitant to begin their long journey. At dusk they are likely to move to a nearby reed-bed to roost for the night. At such times, it is worth keeping an eye open for a Hobby, the small falcon that preys not on mice and voles but on hirundines and large insects such as dragonflies, damselflies, cockchafers and summer chafers. The presence of one will be announced by sharp cries from the Swallows as they rapidly disperse. It is claimed that they have different cries depending upon the predator that they have spotted, effectively shouting "Hobby!" or "Sparrowhawk!" to warn their neighbours.

Every season has its highlights. The arrival of the first summer migrants makes every spring an exciting time. The Brown Hares are engrossed in their ritual battles among the spring corn. Woodpeckers are drumming in the woods, and emerging bright yellow male Brimstones are usually the year's first butterflies. Summer is filled with flowers, butterflies and breeding activity. Autumn sees the replacement of summer migrants from Africa by winter migrants (such as Whooper and Bewick's Swans, wild geese, Fieldfares, Redwings and Bramblings) from the Arctic, Scandinavia and Russia. From mid September onwards, keep an ear open at night for the high-pitched "seep" calls of migrating Redwings, which are usually the first sign of their presence, before they appear in hedgerows and gardens, feeding on haws and *Cotoneaster* or *Pyracantha* berries.

At this time, as the day-length shortens, it seems that some birds confuse autumn with spring, for, suddenly, after being silent for weeks, Willow Warblers, Chiffchaffs and Blackcaps may start to sing somewhat substandard versions of their spring songs. It may be a sad season, as chill mists replace summer's drowsy warmth, but the autumn colours of beech and maple leaves, hips, haws and assorted berries are ample compensation. It is difficult to pick the most interesting and exciting season. That is what makes the English countryside so fascinating, and every walk an adventure. There is always the chance that tomorrow's walk will be the one that produces that unforgettable moment.

First published in *Bedfordshire County Life Magazine* in autumn 2008

Wildlife Puzzle 29
Q. Can you solve these six cryptic clues? The answers are a bird, a butterfly, a dragonfly or damselfly, a plant, a mammal and a moth (not necessarily in that order). 1 Big policeman (5, 6). 2 Emboldened ideals (6, 10). 3 Exclaim "Ow!" joker to follow (6, 7). 4 Portly layer (3-3). 5 Sulphide of mercury (8). 6. Worry (6).

Wildlife Puzzle 30
Q. What is the link between a relative of Gromwell and Blue-eyed Mary; a semi-prostrate member of the pea family with flowers that may be yellow, orange, red, purple, whitish or parti-coloured; and ferns in the genus *Asplenium*?

Wildlife Puzzle 31
Q. Arrange the 16 words in the following list into four groups of four, so that the words in each group have something in common:
Berry Drop Garden Goose Jersey Leopard Pale Purple Ruby Ruff Sand Scarlet Sorrel Vetch Warbler Wood.
There is just one unique solution.

Well I never!

It does not matter how long one has been interested in natural history, there is always something new to see, to find or to learn.

On a recent visit to the flooded gravel-pits at Little Paxton in Cambridgeshire, I was watching the flocks of wintering ducks, which included several diving Goldeneyes amongst the commoner Pochards and Tufted Ducks, and some displaying Smews. There were also groups of surface-feeding or 'dabbling' ducks – Mallards, Gadwalls, Teal and Shovelers. To my great surprise, two of the male Shovelers started to dive. They did this repeatedly, so I timed them, and they consistently remained submerged for 7 seconds. Never before, in over 50 years of birdwatching, had I seen a Shoveler dive in this manner, so, on returning home, I looked up this species' behaviour in various reference books. I discovered, from *The Birds of the Western Palearctic*, that Shovelers feed (1) by surface-feeding, (2) by swimming with head and neck submerged, and (3) by up-ending – as I already knew – but also (4) by "diving, possibly more often than other *Anas*, but still not frequently."

I had thought that I had seen something extraordinary, but I had merely seen behaviour that is infrequent.

By a strange coincidence, only shortly afterwards, when visiting Priory Country Park in Bedford, I came across a group of 66 Shovelers behaving even more oddly. There were 39 males and 27 females in a loose flock at one end of the lake. They were mostly in twos (usually pairs, but sometimes two males), a few trios, a foursome and several singles. They were all swimming in tight circles (pairs following each other, head to tail, and the trios and foursomes similarly following each other head to tail), with their heads submerged. I assumed that they were feeding on organisms stirred up by the eddies and mini-whirlpools caused by their individual or co-operative actions. This peculiar behaviour – which reminded me of the spinning by swimming phalaropes – continued without a break for at least one hour.

Once again, in over 50 years of birdwatching, I had never before seen Shovelers behaving in this manner. David Kramer, however, who watches Priory Park more regularly than anyone else, subsequently told me that he had seen feeding flocks of Shovelers spinning in this manner there on several previous occasions, as had other birdwatchers at other localities. In this case, however, *The Birds of the Western Palearctic* does not describe this communal feeding habit.

On a sunny morning last summer, I watched a well-grown Red Fox cub trotting along the edge of a strip of woodland when it suddenly leapt in the air and turned a somersault. I assumed that it had tried to catch flying prey of some sort, but the cub continued to leap and somersault for several minutes, and I concluded eventually that it was merely 'having fun.' It was delightful to watch, and it is not difficult for us to assume that mammals engage in play, just as we do. What about other animals? Much behaviour by them is explained in terms of the use that it may be to the animal, but there are times when playfulness seems the only logical explanation.

I watched a Blackbird this autumn which repeatedly tossed a large Maple leaf in the air, chased after it and tossed it again, and again, and again. On the first occasions, it was perhaps flicking the leaf aside in order to find food beneath it, but what explanation other than sheer exuberant delight can there be for doing this repeatedly with the same leaf?

The last time that we had a severe frost, I was watching a Blackbird perched on the ridge of a steeply sloping roof when it suddenly slipped forwards and slid down the roof, on its rear end with its head up, as if tobogganing. An accident? If it was, the Blackbird clearly enjoyed the experience, since it flew back up to the roof-ridge and repeated the slide. That must surely have been an example of play? Although I have never seen it myself, I have read about Rooks and other crows perched on wires, holding on and doing complete somersaults until upright again, like an acrobat on a trapeze. There are also accounts of Ravens sliding down icy slopes in the way that Otters play on slippery riverbanks.

What fun it can be for us not merely to identify the creatures that we see in the countryside, but to watch what they are doing.

First published in *Bedfordshire County Life Magazine* in winter 2008/09

Wildlife Puzzle 32
Q. Which is the odd one out from amongst the following: gnu, goat, smew, stoat, teasel, teal, toad, weasel, woad?

Wildlife Puzzle 33
Q. What do Seafheal, the Dunnock or Hedge Accentor or Hedge-sparrow and Basil Fawlty's wife have in common?

Wildlife Puzzle 34
Q. Pair up the 16 words in the following list to make eight names of animals or plants: Bat Bear Bearded Bee Bristly Goat Goat's-beard Moth Moustached Scarlet Spectacled Tiger Tit Warbler Whiskered Willow

From Collared Doves to Coal Tits

We arrived at the church at 04.30, parked our car, got out and closed the doors quietly to avoid waking the still-sleeping villagers. Immediately, we heard the "co-coo-co" of a Collared Dove and the chattering of House Sparrows as they entered and left their nest-holes beneath the tiles of a cottage. One of a pair of Jackdaws perched beside a chimney stack, then disappeared down the chimney, obviously attending their nest. Three species to be entered on our recording card in the first minute. What was this all about?

Currently, birdwatchers throughout Britain and Ireland are taking part in the third survey which will lead to an atlas showing the distribution of all our breeding birds. The previous projects started in 1968 and 1988, so 'snapshots' at 20-year gaps have now become established. To give an idea of what atlas fieldwork can be like, this article describes one morning on the Cambridgeshire-Bedfordshire border.

Three species in the first minute is certainly not unusual. Next came the distant crow of a Pheasant, the repetitious song of a Song Thrush ("he sings each song twice over" according to Browning) and the wheeze of a male Greenfinch from the top of a churchyard yew tree, with another performing his strange bat-like display flight. Yew trees are often home to Goldcrests and Coal Tits, but this time produced just the two commonest tit species, with family parties with fledged young Blue Tits and Great Tits. Half-a-dozen Swifts were flying around the church tower, some entering through ventilator shutters and others screaming overhead in madcap chases.

A footpath led through meadows, past gardens and across cornfields. Wood Pigeons were cooing and, when one crashed noisily out of a bush, its meagre nest was visible against the light of the sky. The distinctive, repeated "ooh-ah" of a cooing Stock Dove, the laughing 'yaffle' of a Green Woodpecker and the sharp "pic" of a Great Spotted Woodpecker came from nearby trees. A series of squeaks revealed a family party of Treecreepers, closely followed by fledged broods of Wrens and Dunnocks. The raucous cries of at least two Jays, the rich song of a Blackcap, and speckled and barely flying fledgling Robins and Blackbirds completed this very productive woodland sortie. After less than half an hour, the recording card already had entries for 20 species, with breeding confirmed for 11 of them.

A field of wheat was unproductive, as is often the case, but thin, piping calls from an overgrown hedge drew attention to a pair of Bullfinches. A "tac" revealed an agitated Lesser Whitethroat, and there was also the quieter "churr" of a Common Whitethroat. It needed only short waits for parents of these two warblers to appear with food in their bills, clearly destined for nestlings or fledglings.

The next field, of barley, was much more productive, with half a dozen Yellowhammers, the males singing their little-bit-of-bread-and-no-cheese songs from the hedgerows, and several scattered pairs of Reed Buntings, some males singing their pathetic, weak songs and one pair going frantic on the path ahead, clearly trying to lure us away from their nest. Midst the cacophony of Sky Larks singing overhead, the jangling song of a distant Corn Bunting was the first real excitement of the day, for this declining species is not always easy to find. At the end of an hour, the total was 27 species, with 14 confirmed breeding.

A Carrion Crow flew to its nest in a hedgerow oak, and Chaffinch, Goldfinch and Linnet then came in quick succession. A farmyard pond held an anxious female Mallard with her downy brood, and the overhanging nettles almost but not quite hid a Moorhen and her fluffy youngsters. A pair of Barn Swallows did as they should (entered a barn, where – with the permission of the farmer – it was easy to find their nest).

Part of the fun of 'atlassing' is the contact with landowners, farmers, keepers and others, for it always pays not merely to ask permission to visit buildings or fields, but also to tap the local knowledge of people who are nearly always interested in the survey and keen to help. In this case, the farmer allowed access to the barn, and also told us where Little Owls could "always be seen" in an old ash tree (they were indeed there) and showed us a Pied Wagtails' nest in an old brick wall. We discovered House Martin nests under the eaves and Starlings carrying food to holes in the roof of another farm building; a female Pheasant led her brood of downy young in single file across the road; and a pair of Red-legged Partridges stood prominently on some straw bales.

Now having the farmer's permission to do so, we investigated a nearby block of woodland and scrub. Magpies and Chiffchaffs were no surprise, but the bonus was a pair of Garden Warblers, with both adults carrying food. The "mew" of a Common Buzzard overhead confirmed that species' presence, and the farmer had told us that they had a nest with young in this wood, so we did not disturb it further.

An adjoining plot of fallow or set-aside, with mixed grass and wild flowers held not only the expected Sky Larks, but also singing Meadow Pipits and that quintessential summer sound, the 'purr' of a Turtle Dove. Once almost commonplace, this has become rare in recent years.

The circular tour back to our car next went between fields

of potatoes and oil-seed rape. Potato fields are now a favoured habitat of Yellow Wagtails that formerly were almost restricted to coastal freshwater marshy fields and flood meadows of river valleys. A scan soon revealed distant brilliant yellow dots and the scarcely audible songs not of Yellowhammers but of Yellow Wagtails. Success! It is very satisfying to spot a habitat, to look for a species and then to find it. One pair obliged by flying closer, with the female carrying food for her young. The oil-seed rape field held not only its expected scattering of Reed Buntings (this is now one of the species' favourite habitats), but also a singing Sedge Warbler.

Almost back to our car, the adult Rooks were noisily attending to well-grown nestlings and fledglings in a rookery. The wooded garden of the nearby rectory looked ideal for Spotted Flycatchers, so, since it was now 09.30 – a perfectly acceptable time to call – we sought and received permission to have a look around. A Spotted Flycatcher appeared – as if on cue – and revealed its nest in the Virginia creeper on the side of the house. Chased by a Sparrowhawk, a Mistle Thrush flashed past, uttering its rattling alarm call. The rector's wife told us that the Mistle Thrushes had reared a brood in the garden earlier in the year, and also that she frequently heard Tawny Owls, and that this year's brood of young owls was still in the garden (she showed us one, roosting in an ivy-clad tree). We thanked her for her kindness and, as we walked back down the drive, a family party of Coal Tits called from a tall conifer, bringing to a splendid conclusion a very successful morning's birding.

We had found 53 species in five hours, and confirmed breeding for 30 of them. This walk through ordinary farmland in summer 2008 was not only a useful five-hour survey, contributing to the county and the national pictures, but had also been enormous fun.

[The magnificent book based on such fieldwork has now been published by BTO Books, Thetford: *Bird Atlas 2007-11. The breeding and wintering birds of Britain and Ireland.* by Dawn Balmer, Simon Gillings, Brian Caffrey, Bob Swann, Iain Downie & Rob Fuller. ISBN 978-1-908581-28-0]

First published in *Bedfordshire County Life Magazine* in spring 2009

Wildlife Puzzle 35
Q. What do the following birds all have in common: Goldeneye, Snow Goose, Great Northern Diver, Sociable Plover and Tawny Pipit?

Wildlife Puzzle 36
Q. What do the buds of the Ash tree, the fruits of Deadly Nightshade and the caterpillars of the Peacock butterfly have in common?

Wildlife Puzzle 37
Q. What do the butterfly *Gonepteryx rhamni*, the plant *Trifolium ochroleucon*, the common fungus *Hypholoma fasciculare* and the moth *Tyria jacobaeae* all have in common?

Wildlife Puzzle 38
Q. What is missing from this selection? *Charaxes jasius* a beautiful Continental and African butterfly, *Bradypus variegatus* the Brown-throated Sloth, *Libellula quadrimaculata* a 'chaser' dragonfly, *Ciliata mustela* the bearded rockling of coastal waters, *Zygaena filipendulae* a common burnet moth, a shooters' and English country name for *Numenius phaeopus* the Whimbrel, *Diloba caeruleocephala* a common late-flying moth, *Amata phegea* a very rare migrant moth, and *Pungitius pungitius* a spined stickleback.

Identification

The first step in the study of any group of animals or plants is to master the identification of the species. Most people are familiar with the birds that visit their gardens and know how to tell a Great Tit from a Blue Tit, but fewer can tell a Mistle Thrush from a Song Thrush and only experienced bird-watchers can distinguish a non-singing Willow Warbler from a Chiffchaff. Even experts have problems sometimes, and in this article I shall recount a few of the biggest blunders made by those who thought that they knew better.

My first story dates back many years, to the late 1940s, when a bird observatory had only recently been established on Fair Isle, the small island lying between Orkney and the mainland of Shetland. The resident warden was Kenneth Williamson and the visitors staying in the hostel-like observatory included the famous (and subsequently infamous) Col. Richard Meinertzhagen. On the day in question, a strange bird had been sighted several times, but it had never been seen for long enough for its identity to be established for certain, and in the latter part of the day, despite a thorough search, the observers had been unable to relocate the bird. After dinner that night, discussion raged. Had they been watching a Short-toed Lark or had it been a Tawny Pipit? The two camps were equally divided, but Col. Meinertzhagen remained aloof from the debate. Eventually, however, his patience was obviously exhausted, for he delved into his pocket and – with the question "Is this the bird that you're talking about?" – drew out his hand holding the corpse of a small sandy-coloured bird. Surreptitiously, the colonel had shot it!

97

That was one way to establish the identity of a mystery bird and, indeed, that was the standard way in the nineteenth century. By the middle of the more-enlightened twentieth century, careful observation, with descriptions and drawings, had replaced the shotgun. Nowadays, the camera and video-camera have, in their turn, almost replaced the notebook in some observers' armoury. Nevertheless, even experts make mistakes.

When I was still at school, I was greatly honoured one day to be invited to go birdwatching with two real experts. At that time, they were my 'gods'. One was the County Bird Recorder and the other was a member of the council of one of the senior ornithological societies, and jointly they were the co-authors of the standard reference book on the birds of the area that we were visiting. I was there to learn from two 'giants'. At one point, they spotted a distant speck out at sea and discussed between themselves whether it was a female Red-breasted Merganser or the very similar female Goosander. I listened in awe as they debated whether the white patch below the bill had diffuse edges (like that on a female Red-breasted Merganser) or was sharply defined (like that on a female Goosander). They were still arguing the point when the creature hauled itself out onto a sandbar and proved to be a Grey Seal. Feet of clay!

The Goosander and another County Bird Recorder both feature in my next tale, too. On this occasion, I was birdwatching at Stewartby Lake just south of Bedford with a close friend who was, at the time, Bedfordshire's Recorder. He spotted a pale object on the far side of the lake and declared that it was a male Goosander. Squinting through my telescope, I disagreed, saying that I was certain that it was merely a discarded plastic bag. The discussion became quite heated, but ended when 'it' swam out from the bank, revealing the bright red bill and glossy-green head possessed by few plastic bags.

My fourth tale involved myself again and the next County Recorder for Bedfordshire (I mention their positions to show that those involved were highly competent observers, not tyros). It was a very hard winter some years prior to our recent freeze in February 2009. As we walked through the working (but currently idle) part of a gravel-pit, we both heard and simultaneously identified the call of a Goldfinch, but could not see one flying overhead. Mystified, we cautiously approached the source of the sound and were amazed to find that it was not a Goldfinch or even a bird, but the sound of drops of water falling from overhead machinery onto the ice covering a puddle. Half-an-hour later, we retuned the same way, and again, simultaneously, remarked "This time, that *is* a Goldfinch!", but it wasn't. Amazingly, we had both been fooled a second time. This sort of experience is why the assessors of bird records are very loath ever to accept 'call-only records'.

My final tale is another similar example, this time involving two experienced observers, but not me personally. During a night-trip in search of nocturnal species – such as Nightjar, Grasshopper Warbler, Corn Crake, Spotted Crake and Nightingale – they heard the distinctive short, soft, deep, far-carrying, regularly repeated "pew" of a Scops Owl. It is well known that the only sound with which this can be confused is the much quieter call of the Midwife Toad (commonly heard from gardens in parts of Bedford). In great excitement, therefore, our two heroes cautiously crept through the woodland, getting closer and closer to the rare owl. Emerging from the wood onto a minor road, they were, however, confronted by the policeman whose motorcycle radio was emitting a short, soft, deep, far-carrying, regularly repeated "pew".

The field-guides don't always mention every pitfall.

First published in *Bedfordshire County Life Magazine* in summer 2009

Wildlife Puzzle 39

Q. What do these animals and plants all have in common? Butterbur; Common Swift; Magpie; Redshank; Sycamore; and Wormwood

Wildlife Puzzle 40

Q. Which of the following plants is the odd one out? Bastard Balm, Bell Heath, Brooklime, Holly, Mezereon, Selfheal and Sweetbriar

Wildlife Puzzle 41

Q. Arrange these 20 birds into five groups of four in such a way that the birds in each group of four have something in common. Brambling, Goldeneye, Common Pheasant, Dipper, Goldfinch, Great Tit, Hoopoe, House Martin, Little Owl, Long-tailed Tit, Mandarin Duck, Lapwing, Northern Wheatear, Nuthatch, Penduline Tit, Red-legged Partridge, Shag, Smew, Waxwing, Wren. There are red herrings, and there is only one unique solution.

Wildlife Puzzle 42

Q. Which of these three plants is the odd one out? Annual Wall-rocket *Diplotaxis muralis*, Bog -myrtle *Myrica gale* and Gladdon *Iris foetidissima*

Did you see the Painted Ladies?

Every so often, there is a wildlife spectacular which occurs near at hand and not in some far-flung part of the world. This year, even inland English counties shared in a mind-boggling event.

Over the Whitsun weekend of 24th-25th May, huge numbers of Painted Lady butterflies were seen flying north. They were easy to miss, since they flew very fast – more like birds than butterflies – storming through, usually below shoulder height, but rising up over hedgerows or trees when these blocked their path, but were an extraordinary sight once noticed.

When the first ones were seen, along the South Coast, the alert went out via telephone and especially e-mail to naturalists farther north, so we were ready for them when they arrived. In my own area, in the valley of the River Ivel, they were streaming past at a mere 360 per hour – roughly one every 10 seconds – but in coastal Norfolk, for instance, there were some 18,000 at a single site, and the arrival rate was about 50 per minute rather than six per minute. This mass migration was observed in every English county, and a simple calculation shows that, if my counts were about average, they were passing north through England at a rate of at least 1 million per hour. Assuming that they passed for ten hours per day on each of the two main days, I calculated that the total had been about 20 million Painted Ladies during the weekend. I was pleased later to find that a more-expertly calculated estimate was 20 million to 50 million. A lot!

Such mass migrations are not annual. In some years, the Painted Lady is quite scarce, and the last big arrival here was in 1996, but the events of 2009 eclipsed anything that I have ever seen before. I even telephoned non-naturalist friends, suggesting that they should go out locally to any piece of open ground (playing fields or town park, for instance) and take a look. The butterflies did not let anyone down. They were everywhere.

This phenomenon was triggered in North Africa by exceptional rainfall in late winter, producing an abundance of the Painted Lady caterpillar's food plants. As a result, tens of thousands of pupae could be seen splitting open and revealing the gorgeously patterned orange butterflies in early spring. These migrated north to Spain, where they bred again, producing the vast numbers that arrived in Britain (and other parts of northern Europe) in May. Now, in late summer and early autumn, we are seeing the new generation of adult butterflies that have been reared in Britain. Here, the caterpillars feed mainly on various thistles, and this is reflected in the specific part of the species' scientific name, *Vanessa cardui*. The British-bred butterflies are beginning to migrate back south again, towards Spain and North Africa. Look now, therefore, for a Painted Lady among the usual Red Admirals, Small Tortoiseshells and Peacocks that frequent the purple flowers of the butterfly bush, *Buddleia*, in gardens and parks on sunny autumn days.

First published in *Bedfordshire County Life Magazine* in autumn 2009

Wildlife Puzzle 43
Q. What is the connection between Adder, Hart and Hound?

Help! Hornets!

A few years ago, seeing a Hornet *Vespa crabro* was very unusual in our part of Britain, being an experience usually confined to foreign holidays or trips to southern places such as the New Forest.

These creatures – our largest species of wasp – look fearsome, being almost twice the length and about five times the bulk of the familiar Common Wasp *Vespula vulgaris* or German Wasp *Vespula germanica*. They are very inquisitive, which makes them seem even more fearsome when a giant yellow-and-black monster comes hurtling towards one's face, perhaps even bumping into one's head. They are, however, 'pussy cats', seldom actually stinging, unlike their smaller cousins.

These days, Hornets have become a much commoner sight here, where they visit flowers in summer (usually seeking flies and other insects, upon which they prey), feast at fallen apples in autumn and frequently come to garden ponds to drink. They can easily be recognised by their large size and distinguished from a large queen of the commoner and smaller species of wasp by their reddish-brown (instead of black) thorax and fore part of the abdomen.

Whereas nests of the smaller wasps can contain hundreds of stinging workers, Hornet nests are usually home to only a few dozen workers. The ball-like, papery nests are made from masticated wood and are usually sited in a crevice such as a hollow tree or a cavity in a wall. When a nest is near a house or footpath, the protective adult insects can present a daunting presence to human passers-by.

Whether in a distant wood or my own garden, I usually

enjoy watching these magnificent insects. Recently, however, I had to search the Yellow Pages and telephone the local council's pest controller with a request that he should attend to a nest in my house. When he arrived in his van and began to don appropriate protective gear, he was far more belligerent than the Hornets. He stated bluntly that he did not want to destroy a Hornets' nest and, indeed, would not do so unless absolutely necessary. I was delighted. What a magnificent – and unexpected – attitude from a council employee, whom one might have expected to have a low opinion of all sorts of what he might have called "vermin". I applauded his very enlightened, modern, conservation-conscious attitude. In the event, he did, however, need to poison the Hornets and block up the entrance to their nest, since it was a mere metre away from the front door of my house. The Hornets had given a scare to the postman and various other visitors, and although – luckily – no-one had actually been stung, there was the risk that someone would be, and a single Hornet sting can be very painful, several even more so.

If you see a Hornet, do treasure the experience. If you don't harass it, it's exceedingly unlikely to harm you. They are gentle giants.

First published in *Bedfordshire County Life Magazine* in winter 2009/10

Wildlife Puzzle 44
Q. What do the Daddy-longlegs Spider *Pholcus phalangioides*, the King Cobra *Ophiophagus hannah* and the Sparrowhawk *Accipiter nisus* have in common?

'Bare winter suddenly was changed to spring'

This quote from *The Question* by Shelley seems particularly apt this year, after the harshest winter in our county for over 30 years. Ponds and lakes were covered in ice, with just a few areas of open water on some of the largest, resulting in an exodus of many wildfowl and concentrations of those that remained into milling flocks. With the ground frozen solid, birds that usually probe in the soil or mud were also under severe pressure. Attempting to escape the big freeze, a few Lapwings even managed to reach eastern North America. How many thousands must have perished in their attempt to cross the North Atlantic? Along the English south coast, tens of thousands of Sky Larks and 'winter thrushes' (the Fieldfares and Redwings that breed in northern continental Europe but overwinter in Britain and Ireland) poured eastwards in what are referred to as hard-weather movements or snow-migration. They were trying to escape the harsh conditions in Ireland and western Britain, but were unknowingly heading straight into even worse conditions in southeastern England, northern France and the Low Countries. The snow and freezing conditions lasted for a far shorter period than in the infamous winter of 1962/63, so perhaps many of these weather-refugees may have survived. Breeding-bird censuses in their breeding areas may tell us later this year.

Some of these at-risk birds did try to stay, but the thrushes soon stripped the berried trees and bushes and mostly moved on. Here and there, it was possible to come across a Snipe or a Woodcock feeding in the soft mud beside a slightly-above-freezing brook, but most had moved to try to find milder conditions. Similarly, Fieldfares, Redwings and Song Thrushes mostly departed, but Blackbirds were much in evidence throughout the snow, scuffling along with the Pheasants amongst the piles of dead leaves beneath hedgerows, and appeared to be finding enough food to survive the freeze.

Many human beings helped by providing food in their gardens, and it was noticeable when walking in the snow that there were far more birds in villages and the suburbs of towns than in the open countryside. The woods were silent, desolate places. The birds that suffer the greatest losses in these conditions are those that are strictly insectivorous, such as Wrens, Goldcrests and Treecreepers, and which never (or only very rarely) come to the food provided at bird-tables. A few decades ago, Long-tailed Tits would have been in that list of at-hazard species, but in recent years some have aped the behaviour of Blue, Great and Coal Tits by feeding on the peanuts and other food in hanging containers, and this may have helped them to survive the winter. Summer censuses will reveal the effectiveness of this help.

So now it is spring. Mistle Thrushes will have been singing since December and may now already have fledglings, and so too will early-nesting Blackbirds and Song Thrushes. The effects of the winter may have reduced the numbers of particularly vulnerable species, but they will soon recover, for those at most risk usually are also those which have the largest clutches of eggs and broods of nestlings. Wrens may have five or six eggs and rear two broods each year, so two in spring could become fourteen by late summer; if as many as ten of these die in the next six months, the population will still have doubled by the following spring. Goldcrests also have two broods, and usually lay seven or eight eggs, so numbers can be restored even more quickly. Events that are a catastrophe for the individual are not necessarily a major setback for the species.

By late March, the first returning summer migrants will be back, the Chiffchaff's repetitive "chiff chaff chiff chaff" often being the first evidence, adding to the chorus dominated by the Great Tit's loud "tea-cher!" and the melodious songs of Blackbird and Song Thrush. Then there's the buzz of a low-flying Sand Martin, the chirruping calls of Swallows, and House Martins are again investigating nest-sites below the eaves of favoured houses. Hear the first distant "cuck-oo" and it will soon be summer.

First published in *Bedfordshire County Life Magazine* in spring 2010

Wildlife Puzzle 45
Q. Which of these 12 names is the odd one out? Badger, Bunting, Fox, Mole, Snipe, Squirrel, Stoat, Thrush, Tit, Vole, Weasel, Wren

Wildlife Puzzle 46
Q. Find the flower and the six birds in these anagrams: Cranky Lobby, Octave, Ornate Trees, Pines, Regret Badge Secret, Shorn Thugs & Workload.

What's that hawk?

There is a special fascination provided by birds of prey. Whereas all the 'little brown birds' skulk in bushes and are regarded as being impossible to identify, the raptors tend to make themselves obvious. Thus, the questions posed by interested non-experts are often in the form "I saw a hawk yesterday. What was it?"

In these days, now that keepers and landowners are far more enlightened than in the nineteenth and early twentieth centuries, there are plenty of possible candidates in our part of Britain. The best clue is usually provided not by the bird's plumage or even its size and shape, but by its behaviour.

Was it hovering on rapidly beating wings, or hanging in an up-draught on barely wavering wings? "Yes" and it was almost certainly a Kestrel, hunting for voles or mice. Common Buzzards do hover sometimes, but are much clumsier, larger and have broad wings in contrast to the Kestrel's narrow, pointed wings.

If the bird was sitting on top of a telegraph pole or the top of a tree or bush, the same two species are the most likely options. Twenty years ago, Common Buzzards were almost unknown here, being largely confined to the north and west of Britain, but these days they are as common as or sometimes even commoner than Kestrels, having spread rapidly and naturally back to their former haunts. Common Buzzards feed largely on rabbits, so tend to sit around in trees for long periods and then suddenly glide down towards their target prey.

"I was standing in the garden and this hawk swept past me at shoulder height and then vanished over the fence, scattering all the small birds from the bird-table..." Far commoner than they were, also having benefited from the more benign attitude of those who rear and shoot game-birds, Sparrowhawks may now even appear in suburbia. Their hunting technique comprises a swift, low-level flight, swooping over hedgerows and around bushes to surprise and ambush small birds unaware of their approach.

"I looked up and there was a bird-of-prey gliding slowly in circles high up in the sky. What was it?" Most raptors occasionally take advantage of thermals to gain height, but – if they are not too high or if a pair of binoculars is handy – they then give us the opportunity to see their distinctive shapes. Most raptors are far easier to identify when in flight than when perched. The most frequent circling raptor is the Common Buzzard, with its broad wings and relatively short tail. They also often draw attention to themselves by uttering a cat-like "mew". Sparrowhawks also frequently soar in thermals, when their very rounded wings and relatively long tail distinguish them easily from the Kestrels, which also have long tails, but have pointed wings.

As a result of the re-establishment of Red Kites in Oxfordshire and Northamptonshire, individuals from those centres of population have now spread and even begun to breed in our area. We now, therefore, do not need to travel to central Wales to see the magnificent sight of one of these long-winged, long-tailed birds sailing overhead. Look for the distinctive, deeply notched or forked tail, which is used as a rudder, twisting and turning as the bird manoeuvres effortlessly overhead. Like Common Buzzards, these carrion feeders tend to spend long periods hidden away, perched in trees, when they are not circling high in the sky.

A further ten species of raptor might be seen here: Honey-buzzard; Marsh, Hen and Montagu's Harriers; Goshawk; Rough-legged Buzzard; Osprey; Merlin, Hobby and Peregrine Falcon. They are all sufficiently rare to excite even avid birdwatchers, and only the last of them, the Peregrine Falcon, is likely to be spotted by the casual observer. Once confined almost entirely to coastal cliffs and remote rocky areas such as mountains and quarries, a few Peregrines have now taken to frequenting man-made cliffs, such as the windowsills and ledges on high-rise buildings in city centres. If you are lucky enough to see a stocky falcon attempting to catch a feral Rock Dove (a 'Town Pigeon'), you can be pretty sure that it was a Peregrine Falcon.

Gone are the days when the only raptor likely to be seen here was the Kestrel. The recovery from the low point in the 1950s – when pesticide poisoning exacerbated the effects of excessive predator control – has been dramatic, especially in the past couple of decades.

To pre-empt an inevitable question: no, we do not need to be concerned that this increase in numbers of raptors will result in a decline in the populations of common song-birds. These avian predators take relatively few, and naturally prey upon the slowest, least agile and least alert individuals. Natural selection in action!

First published in *Bedfordshire County Life Magazine* in summer 2010

Wildlife Puzzle 47

Q. What is also known as Biddy's-eyes, Come-and-cuddle-me, Jack-jump-up-and-kiss-me, Kiss-her-in-the-buttery, Kiss-me-quick, Love-in-idleness, Three-faces-in-a-hood and Tickle-my-fancy?

Surprises and anticipation

The wonderful thing about being a general naturalist (or, to put it more simply, someone with an interest in several or all aspects of natural history) is that there is almost always something that transforms a walk into an adventure.

This last summer, for instance, I visited a small, isolated wood, hoping to find breeding Blackcap, Garden Warbler and, perhaps, Nuthatch. Two out of three was a satisfactory result, but even better was a wonderful display of hundreds of metre-high flowering stems of Spiked Star of Bethlehem, topped with their delicate white blooms. This striking plant is found in only a few places in our region. Then, elated by that discovery, and walking along an overgrown footpath around the edge of the same wood, ten heads popped up from the long grass. Not Pheasants or even Red-legged or Grey Partridges, but a little party of Helmeted Guineafowl. This introduced species is native to North Africa, but is bidding (along with Indian Peafowl) to join American Grey Squirrel, Chinese Muntjac and Asian Rose-ringed Parakeet, among others, as an established alien in the United Kingdom.

Early on another morning, I was driving on deserted roads to start a survey of the birds on an arable farm when an exquisite dark shape looped elegantly across the road in front of the car. Far bigger than a Weasel, larger even than the largest Stoat, this hump-backed mammal was only the second Polecat that I have ever seen in Eastern England. Not long ago, this species was confined to Wales, but – like the Common Buzzard and the Raven – has expanded its range eastwards, back into the territory from which it was exterminated in the nineteenth century by over-enthusiastic game-preservation interests demanding the elimination of almost all predators.

On a third occasion, my companions and I were visiting a wood, hoping to find White Admiral, Purple Hairstreak and Purple Emperor butterflies. We succeeded with only the first of these, but even more exciting was the discovery of a huge patch of the elegant, bobble-headed Small Teasel. There were, perhaps, 200 or 300 plants, in an area where the county's expert botanists had never found it. New colonists or previously overlooked? Surely the former.

My last example took place during a trip totally unrelated to natural history. We were engaged in a name-the-scarecrow competition in aid of charity when a clump of Red Valerian was visited by a Hummingbird Hawk-moth, its whirring wings beating so fast that they were just a blur, making it, indeed, look just like a hummingbird. With its striking black-and-white abdomen and orange-patched wings, this delightful migrant moth entranced several other people similarly looking for the scattered scarecrows. Totally unexpected, but a delightful highlight of the day.

Now that autumn is here, breeding-bird surveys and butterfly counts will come to an end, to be replaced by dawn watches of counts of migrating birds. What will make these memorable this year? It is the unexpected highlights that make these early morning watches so addictive. If the results were predictable, there would be far less incentive to rise on a dark, cold autumn morning and sit or stand for a couple of hours on a dewy or frosty hillside. One year, there were hundreds of Jays; in another, thousands of tits; and, in a third, huge flocks of Common Cranes. Wood Pigeons pour south every year, but the sight of thousands storming past in vast flocks is still spectacular. Likewise, the winter thrushes

(Redwings and Fieldfares), Chaffinches and Bramblings from Fenno-Scandia and Eastern Europe always put on a good show, although coinciding with the actual date when huge numbers fly past necessitates spending many birdless dawns full of unfulfilled expectations. What unexpected companions will these flocks contain this year? I can't wait!

First published in *Bedfordshire County Life Magazine* in autumn 2010

Wildlife Puzzle 48
Q. The start of a very smart tree, a consumed tree and a winged tree show what they all have. What is that?

Wildlife Puzzle 49
Q. Which of these four butterflies is the odd one out? Camberwell Beauty, Painted Lady, Peacock and Clouded Yellow

Waxwings and Wood Pigeons

Every so often, the autumn berry crop in Britain is feasted upon not only by the regular Blackbirds, Redwings, Fieldfares and Mistle Thrushes, but also by exotic Bohemian Waxwings. Arriving in October and November, these Starling-sized birds also look like Starlings when in flight, with triangular-shaped wings and rather short, square-ended tails. When perched, however, they reveal the features that distinguish them from every other European bird. The crown feathers are raised in a crest and the secondary wing feathers have red, waxy tips from which the species gets its name. The plumage is mainly a mixture of soft browns and greys, ranging from deep mahogany to pale chestnut and smoky grey. Add bright yellow-and-white edges to the primary wing feathers, a black chin and black mask through the eye, and a broad yellow tip to the tail, and the resulting bird looks as if it would be more at home in a tropical aviary than in the English countryside. They often come in flocks and love to feed on autumn berries, including those on garden plants such as *Cotoneaster* and *Pyracantha*, so are frequently seen by members of the public who have no special interest in birds, but who want to know about these striking and distinctive strangers.

This year is a 'Waxwing year'. Large numbers arrived on the Scottish and English East Coast and many penetrated inland as far as our area. While berries remain on the bushes for them to eat, they will probably stay around to be seen and enjoyed by birdwatchers and those lucky enough to have them in their gardens. Why do they come in some years and not others? It is, again, all tied up with food supply. When there is plenty of natural food in Russia and Fenno-Scandia, they move only a short distance in autumn, but, if food is in short supply, they fly farther south and west and even cross the North Sea to invade our shores. If this food shortage occurs after a particularly successful breeding season, the numbers may be huge.

Speaking of huge numbers, this last autumn saw the largest diurnal passage of migrants observed here in recent years. The birds involved were mainly Wood Pigeons, which are not generally thought of as migrants. The 'big day' was 7th November, when a record total of over 161,257 Wood Pigeons was counted passing the watchpoint at Constitution Hill, Poole, Dorset, in four hours. The observers there commented that "It was hard to keep an accurate count and numbers will have been underestimated because of the sheer volume of birds across a broad vista. Wood Pigeon numbers split by hour 16,547, 42,000, 58,000, 44,710." This huge passage was also noted at several other sites in Hampshire, Dorset and Devon, and also in the Pennines. The observers at Oxenhope, Bradford, West Yorkshire, for instance, who recorded 19,737 in seven and a half hours, described the scene: "To us overlooking the Bradford skies from high in the west ... in absolutely ideal viewing conditions ... we could see Wood Pigeon flocks at all ranges and all heights for a very lengthy period this morning ... at peak we had never seen the skies so thick with 'pigs', all pounding south, big flocks, small flocks, tight balls, long ovals, even thick cigars."

It was just as spectacular in our area, with 13,795 Wood Pigeons passing over my own watchpoint at Sharpenhoe Clappers in Bedfordshire, for instance. There, I wrote: "Tremendous Wood Pigeon passage ... but I gave up after 90 minutes through sheer fatigue of non-stop counting and writing. So busy that I had to count and remember three flocks, write them down, count and remember three more flocks, write them down, and so on. Passing at all heights from hilltop level to so high that they were just dots. Total of 190 flocks (2-210, average 73). All going NE to SW, so coming at me at an angle (Wood Pigeons usually pass N to S). When I was counting flocks to the right, I could hear flocks whooshing past directly overhead and when I looked left there were flocks there too, so I must have missed at least 20% if not 50% of what was passing. It needed 2 or 3 people to make a thorough count." It was some of the most exciting birdwatching that I have ever experienced.

Where were these Wood Pigeons coming from? And where were they going? Fascinatingly, we do not know. The Wood Pigeon is a serious agricultural pest, so these mass movements have been the subject of considerable professional study over the years. There is, however, scant evidence of large numbers ever crossing the North Sea, although researchers have investigated this for over 50 years. Similarly, although flocks have been watched flying out to sea from the English South Coast, they or others have also been seen coming in or returning. Do they come from Scotland and Northern England or from Scandinavia? Do they go to France and Iberia or do they mostly stay in Britain and perhaps Ireland? Two mysteries still to be solved.

If you want to see full details of these and other observations of migration in Britain and the near Continent, you can browse on the internet on a marvellous Dutch site: www.trektellen.nl

First published in *Bedfordshire County Life Magazine* in winter 2010/11

Surveys and censuses

This spring and summer will see the completion of the five years of fieldwork for the mapping of the breeding and wintering distributions of the birds of Britain and Ireland. Co-ordinated by the British Trust for Ornithology, BirdWatch Ireland and the Scottish Ornithologists' Club, this mammoth task has involved about 30,000 ordinary birdwatchers searching for, counting and recording all the birds within some 90,000 2-km x 2-km squares (known as tetrads). Previous articles in this book have described the ways in which this fieldwork is being carried out and the enjoyment and excitements experienced by participants [and the resulting 720-page *Bird Atlas 2007-11* has now been published, ISBN 978-1-908581-28-0].

The mapping and counting of all our birds, common as well as rare, has been carried out only in the past 60 years or so, starting on a small scale with the Common Bird Census. Just a few dozen expert amateurs each made a detailed study of a small area of farmland, their results being analysed and interpreted by a team of professionals at the BTO and extrapolated in an attempt to show year-to-year population trends in the United Kingdom. That census has now evolved into several more-accurate sample census schemes, such as the Breeding Bird Survey, carried out by many more observers in randomly selected 1-km x 1-km squares.

Previously, the limited manpower available was insufficient for censuses and surveys to cover the whole spectrum of birds, so individual species were targeted. A census of the colonies of Grey Herons has been carried out annually since 1928, and a wide range of species – generally the scarcer ones, such as Black Redstart, Little Ringed Plover and Great Crested Grebe – have been the subject of periodic counts. A census of the last of those species provides a tale from the past that has already appeared in print (*The Hobby* 100: 5-6), but which deserves to be retold. It involves one of our most famous ornithologists, the late Max Nicholson, the instigator of many important projects and the first Director-General of the Nature Conservancy.

I got to know the great Max Nicholson well only in the closing years of his life, in the 1990s, when he was in his eighties, but it was always a delight when he visited me, since he was a fund of amusing, instructive and scandalous stories about birdwatching incidents, events and people. One story that he related concerned himself and our own part of East Anglia. I can verify few of the facts and can only pass on the story told to me by Max as I remember it. Max himself found it amusing, so, as you read it, think of this august man sitting in an armchair recounting and chuckling about events that occurred some 80 years ago.

"Barely out of school, I found myself responsible for collating reports of breeding Great Crested Grebes in Oxfordshire, Berkshire, Bedfordshire and neighbouring counties, as part of a national census. Numbers had increased from the all-time low of about 40 pairs in the whole of Britain in 1860, but it was still a very rare bird. Only a handful of pairs were known in the whole of Bedfordshire when I received a postcard – sent by the Duchess herself – informing me that several pairs, almost doubling the previous total, had nested on the lakes in Woburn Park.

"Who was I to query a record from the Duchess? But such an unusual report needed to be verified. Surreptitiously, therefore, I entered the grounds of the Park and crept up to the lake. There, indeed, were the reported grebes, just as the Duchess had described. Also, however, there was a line of keepers with dogs and guns advancing towards me across the lawns. A shout of 'Hey, you!' showed that I had been spotted. I could not allow myself to be caught – trespassing and, therefore, obviously having doubted the Duchess's word – so I tried to escape capture, pursued by a throng of irate keepers and barking dogs.

"Unfortunately, a 12-foot-high fence barred my way, but I leapt onto it, scrambled over and dropped to the other side, only to be confronted by an irate Wildebeest.

"Even more quickly, I exited that paddock, via another 12-foot fence. To my horror, I had, however, merely transferred to a second paddock, which contained another Wildebeest, so I had to clamber up yet another 12-foot fence. I was out of breath and exhausted, but very relieved to have escaped not only from the two Wildebeests, but also, especially, from the line of similarly irate keepers. Integrity intact, I slunk back home, to pen a thank-you letter to the Duchess."

[The cartoon is by Nick Sinden.]

First published in *Bedfordshire County Life Magazine* in spring 2011

119

Out of synch

This has been an amazing spring, following an exceptional winter. Deep snow and freezing conditions in December delighted the children, but were not good news for wildlife. We were again surprised in April, with no rain until the closing days of the month, and temperatures rising sometimes to those that we expect in midsummer.

Many plants responded to the drought with some of the best displays of flowers in living memory, and the sudden onset of high temperatures triggered growth and flowering ahead of schedule for some plants, so that the countryside looked like a mixture of March, April and May combined. Gardens had Snowdrops and flowering Cherries, Daffodils and Lilies of the Valley, Aconites and Bluebells, Lesser Celandines and Cowslips all appearing simultaneously, the early species on time and the later ones very early. Native plants, including trees, as well as cultivated garden plants reacted similarly. So did some animals, especially insects, with bumblebees, bee-flies and butterflies appearing earlier and sometimes in larger numbers than usual. Red Admirals, Peacocks, Commas, Brimstones, Orange-tips, Green-veined Whites and Holly Blues could be seen in many gardens.

Except in a few marshy areas, the ground, however, was rock hard, which must have made it difficult for birds such as Blackbirds to find food for their nestlings. Many – perhaps most – birds time their breeding so that their nestlings coincide with the peak in their favourite prey species. The best-known example is probably the Blue Tit, its nestlings being fed mainly on caterpillars found on Oaks. Thus, if the food is early and the nestlings are on time, the parents will have difficulty rearing the brood. That was the case this year, with Oaks in leaf earlier than usual.

Migrants clearly reacted to weather conditions farther south, in the Mediterranean and North African regions, for some came very early this year. For birdwatchers, mid April was more like early May, just as it had been for gardeners and botanists.

This was the pattern in our part of England, but the news everywhere seems to have been of unusual timing, with some parts of the World suffering unusual deluges and floods, but others suffering exceptional droughts. Rice could not be planted both because the ground was bone-dry and because it was under metres of water. News bulletins seemed filled with such examples of contrasting disasters. Even sceptics must be becoming aware that global climate change is not a myth. Unfortunately, whereas scientists think in decades, centuries, millennia and eons, politicians still generally think only as far as the next election. It is also not convenient for politicians to accept that one cause – perhaps the major cause – of global climate change is human activity, and that failure to take drastic action is not an option. The World's current problems will seem ridiculously trivial if some predictions of climate change come to pass. Human-beings could face the same problems as the Blue Tits; the great wheatlands could face the same problems as are being suffered by some Asian rice farmers. Rise in sea level could engulf some entire countries. The risk of diversion or cessation of the Gulf Stream has been mooted, giving Western Europe arctic winters, or even triggering another Ice Age. When this last occurred, Human-beings merely migrated south to a more hospitable climate zone. Now, however, there are national borders, passports and visas ...

We have strayed far from the story of our glorious spring, but what we have seen in our own gardens is not just a display of lovely flowers, butterflies and birds, but also a warning.

First published in *Bedfordshire County Life Magazine* in summer 2011

Wildlife Puzzle 50
Q. If you picked the odd one out from among bee, butterfly, fly, frog, lark, lizard, monkey and spider, and the odd one out from among desert, garden, hill, marsh, reed, river, sedge, willow and wood, where would you be in Bedfordshire?

End of an era

It's all over! The summer of 2011 saw the final season of the mammoth distribution survey of the breeding and wintering birds of Britain and Ireland, which we have featured every now and again in these pages. The surveys have been organised nationally by the British Trust for Ornithology, the Scottish Ornithologists' Club and BirdWatch Ireland, but run locally by the county bird clubs. Many thousands of birdwatchers have contributed records, which are displayed in the familiar dot-distribution maps. When the numerical data are analysed, there will also be maps showing the relative numbers. With previous national projects in the breeding seasons of 1968-72 and 1988-91, and the winters of 1981-84, it is now possible to begin to assess the changes that have occurred. It is clear that they have been remarkably numerous and remarkably extensive. The full details will eventually be available in the publication of national and local atlases, but some snippets can already whet our appetites.

There were numerous range expansions between the first and second breeding bird atlases, and some (such as that of the Common Buzzard) have continued or even accelerated, whereas others (such as that of the Nuthatch) seem to have reached a temporary maximum or to have faltered. There have been some stunning new range expansions, such as those of Raven, Little Egret and Oystercatcher. These are all natural changes, effected by changing conditions (climate, habitat and response to reduced direct human intervention). The increase in Red Kites in our area is, of course, a result of the re-establishment programmes in the close-by counties of Oxfordshire and Northamptonshire.

There have also been some striking natural declines or reductions in range, with Tree Sparrows, Tree Pipits, Lesser Spotted Woodpeckers and Lesser Redpolls disappearing from many of their former haunts. Woodcocks and Nightingales are fewer, and, as an extreme example, the Willow Tit is probably now extinct in both Bedfordshire and Cambridgeshire, and heading towards extinction in Northamptonshire.

Birdwatchers would have known about all these changes even without the recent massive co-operative fieldwork exercise. It is, however, the more subtle changes which are, perhaps, the most fascinating, and these are sometimes shown most clearly in the local surveys (based on 2-km x 2-km squares rather than the coarser 10-km x 10-km squares of the National scheme). It seems that Meadow Pipits have expanded considerably in our part of lowland Eastern England, from largely grassland areas, such as those on chalk and heathland, into arable agricultural farmland. This would surely not have been noticed without careful survey work? Similarly, Yellow Wagtails have continued to spread away from their traditional water-meadows of the river valleys into arable crops, such as wheat and potatoes, even in the uplands. In the same way, breeding Reed Buntings are now sometimes easier to find in fields of oil-seed rape than they are along streams and ditches. The ranges of even common-or-garden species such as the Starling and House Sparrow have contracted.

The increase in artificially created (or restored) wetland areas has certainly been beneficial to some waders, with Oystercatchers colonising in the past couple of decades, and even Avocets beginning to gain a foothold.

[The national distribution and abundance maps for the

latest survey are compared with the results from the previous atlas surveys in the gigantic and magnificent tome *Bird Atlas 2007-11*, published by BTO Books in 2013.]

What will we all do next? There will doubtless be new surveys, to look in more detail at species which have declined (Woodcock and Nightingale are obvious prime examples), but for many avid 'atlassers' it will be a long wait for the next national survey, probably now 20 years in the future. The recent changes were not predicted back in the 1970s or 1990s, so it is idle to speculate on the changes that will occur between now and 2030. There is little doubt, however, that – if we did know them now – we would be amazed, with some species that are now common having declined or disappeared and others that are currently totally unknown having colonised. Change is far quicker than anyone imagined just a few decades ago.

First published in *Bedfordshire County Life Magazine* in autumn 2011

Wildlife Puzzle 51

Q. Dock Field Garlic Penny-cress Sandpiper Vole Water White Wood

Using eight of these nine words (six of them twice and two of them once), construct the names of seven British animals and plants and put them into a chain that leads from a plant to an insect, with each adjoining species sharing part of the name of those next to it in the chain (e.g. Marsh Sow-thistle to Marsh Warbler to Grasshopper Warbler to Meadow Grasshopper). Which word is not used in the chain?

Highlights

I can look back now over some 60 years of natural history encounters. By picking out the highlights, I can, perhaps, point readers, most of who will be younger than myself, in directions so that they can also experience similar wonders.

Back in autumn 1959, I undertook the long journey, via Fishguard in Pembrokeshire, on the MV *Innisfallen* across the Irish Sea to Cork City, by train to Skibbereen, then by bus to Baltimore and finally on the mailboat *Naomh Ciaron* across Roaringwater Bay, to the then-remote island of Cape Clear, the southwesternmost tip of Ireland (apart from the Fastnet Rock, four miles offshore). I spent 11 weeks on the island that autumn, investigating its potential as a new bird observatory in the chain of such establishments around the coasts of Britain and Ireland, which then numbered less than a dozen. It proved to be more than worthy, was officially recognised by the British Trust for Ornithology in the following year, and is still going strong now, over 50 years later, with accommodation for visiting naturalists and counts of its migrants and resident birds, butterflies and other wildlife maintained daily.

Watching the same area day after day will always reveal interesting changes as the seasons progress, and sometimes astounding differences from one year to the next. This 'patch watching' does not need to be in some distant place; it can be a local park, nearby farmland or even one's own garden. Inevitably, interesting things will be seen – a migrant Hummingbird Hawk-moth, a Great Spotted Woodpecker teaching its newly fledged youngster how to feed for itself or a Blackbird taking advantage of a Mole's burrowings to snatch worms. But keeping a daily diary of what can be observed will, in time, reveal the changes that pose intriguing questions.

My stay on Cape Clear Island gave me a love for the island, its people and Ireland, so that I returned year after year. Some of my most exciting wildlife encounters were there. Three involved sightings during seawatches (timed counts of passing seabirds). On one occasion, I saw a tall, dark, vertical object surging through the water, and my first thought was that it must be the periscope of a submarine. No, it was, of course, the two-metre-high dorsal fin of a male Killer Whale, revealed by its striking black-and-white patterning. It was leading a small pod of smaller females and youngsters, the first of several sightings over the years of these magnificent predators.

I made a fool of myself (though I was alone so was never mocked) on another occasion. About a mile offshore, a huge animal suddenly launched itself vertically almost wholly out of the sea, with long appendages dangling down at its sides. My instant thought was that it must be an enormous Giant Squid, the appendages being its tentacles, but I then realised that this was another whale, breaching, and that the appendages were its flippers, their immense length showing that it was a Humpback Whale. At that time, this was a totally unexpected sighting, since, according to expert published opinion, "Humpback Whales do not occur in the eastern North Atlantic."

My third encounter was when I was sitting on rocks right beside the sea. Two Risso's Dolphins appeared just offshore, and they clearly saw me. These are big, bulky dolphins, almost twice the length of a Common Dolphin, with a blunt head. These two apparently decided to try to intimidate me (or play a game with me, perhaps) and they came charging straight at me through the sea, coming to a halt only just beyond my hastily retracted feet. It was indeed intimidating to face the equivalent of two large charging marine bulls. They continued to charge at me until, I assume, they got bored. These are just the three most thrilling of many encounters with cetaceans. Passing whales proved to be regular, though were usually seen only in calm conditions.

Even the most avid birdwatchers tend to stop looking at birds when there is a passing whale. Many years later, I was invited to join a friend on a whale-watching cruise from San Diego down the Mexican coast of Baya California and into the Sea of Cortez. If you get the chance yourself, do it! We connected scores of times with a dozen species of cetacean, including close encounters with Blue Whales, the largest animal ever known on Earth, and even closer encounters with Grey Whales. A lagoon there is the nursery of Grey Whales, the females and their calves staying in this safe environment before taking their youngsters on the long and perilous journey to Polar waters. Since the cessation of whaling, some of these Grey Whales have become almost tame, and approach Human-beings in small boats, allowing themselves (and encouraging their calves) to be stroked. To have a gigantic whale coming to be petted, and, indeed, insisting that it receives attention, is a wonderful experience. My trip was with the expert-accompanied wildlife travel group WildWings (visit wildwings.co.uk) on a small boat with only about 30 passengers and crew. Organised commercial trips such as this are often the best way to see such wildlife spectaculars, and the companies concerned are always very happy to send brochures to prospective participants. As well as not having to worry about the itinerary details, the other advantage is that you know that all your companions will have a similar interest and that there will be abundant expertise available to supply the answers to one's questions. Trips like this can be expensive, but are once-in-a-lifetime experiences.

In a future article, I shall describe a few more of the highlights of my travels worldwide, including Mountain Gorillas in Rwanda, birdwatching trips with the Sandy-based travel company Sunbird (visit www.sunbirdtours.co.uk), and the coral reefs of my second-favourite country, Thailand.

First published in *Bedfordshire County Life Magazine* in winter 2011/12

Wildlife Puzzle 52
Q. If a 29 could be Small or Large as it flies by, a 47 something bears catkins, and a 79 finch enjoys Teasel seeds, would you be more likely to see 16 Tuft or a Spotted 16 in Bedfordshire?

Where shall we go for a walk?

With winter over and some calmer, warmer, drier days, it is in spring that many of us think of a countryside stroll. Our region is blessed with many footpaths, and by consulting a map it is easy to plot a pleasant circular walk. By targeting a well-known wildlife area, we can be assured of an even-more-interesting expedition.

Our area is dotted with reserves managed by the Bedfordshire, Cambridgeshire and Northamptonshire Wildlife Trust. Each one has its own unique character and, generally, one or more special attractions – a rare habitat or rare species with very specific soil and climatic requirements. There are no fewer than 99 to choose from – 40 in Cambridgeshire, 23 in Bedfordshire and 36 in Northamptonshire – but I have selected six to show the sorts of places that are within easy reach, and the range of interesting features that they contain.

The Beechwoods reserve just three miles from the centre of Cambridge is just that, a small wood of mature Beech trees. It is a favoured spot in some winters for flocks of Bramblings feeding on the beech-mast. They are the northern equivalent of our Chaffinch, and some stay into April or even May in some years, before migrating back to Fenno-Scandia or Russia. They may be difficult to spot until they move, since their plumage is superbly camouflaged against the black, brown, gold and orange of the bare ground, fallen leaves and shadows. In spring, the generally open woodland floor of this beechwood is sprinkled with the delicate white flower spikes of an orchid, White Helleborine. (Map reference TL485547)

The 900-year-old Brampton Wood between Brampton and Grafham is one of the few localities where the very rare Black Hairstreak may be found. Restricted in the United Kingdom to just a scatter of sites in central England, this butterfly can be seen only in a very short period during mid June to mid July. Although the caterpillar's food-plant is Blackthorn, the butterflies themselves usually frequent the tops of tall trees, feeding on honey-dew, but are observed most easily when they venture lower, to feed on the nectar of Bramble, Privet or Wayfaring-tree flowers. (TL184698)

Some seven miles northwest of Bedford, the Felmersham reserve consists largely of gravel excavations flooded over 50 years ago and now very well vegetated. It is, perhaps, most renowned for the wide range of dragonflies and damselflies that can be seen there. At least 18 species breed on the reserve, and others occur along the nearby River Great Ouse. Among the many interesting plants, the orange-yellow flowers of Bladderwort can sometimes make a spectacular display in summer on the small pools. This floating plant is one of our few so-called insectivorous species, though its underwater bladders trap and then digest any tiny swimming creature, not just insects. The reserve is also a magnet for migrant birds in spring, often hosting the earliest Chiffchaffs, Willow Warblers and Sedge Warblers. (SP991584)

Perhaps Bedfordshire's most intriguing reserve, Flitwick Moor consists of wooded iron-rich peaty pools and fast-flowing streams encrusted with orange ferric-oxide. If you are lucky, you may hear the pig-like squealing of Water Rails in spring and summer as well as in winter. It is also one of the best places to hear or see the tiny sparrow-sized Lesser Spotted Woodpecker, which has disappeared from many other former sites in our area. It is remarkable botanically, with, for instance, as many as nine different species of *Sphagnum* moss. In spring, look for carpets of the rare Opposite-leaved Golden-saxifrage, the flowers of which lack petals but have bright yellow sepals. In autumn, fungi include everyone's favourite, the poisonous Fly Agaric, with its red cap covered with white spots, featured so often in illustrations of fairies and gnomes. (TL046354)

Hayley Wood lies less than four miles east of Gamlingay. Like nearby Potton Wood, it is on boulder clay and is one of the best places to go in spring to see the very local Oxlip. This resembles a large-flowered Cowslip, so it is necessary to distinguish it carefully from the occasional hybrid Primrose x Cowslip. These woods are home to the native Roe Deer as well as the introduced Muntjac. (TL292530)

Reserves are not always in the middle of the countryside. That at The Riddy is right beside the A1, just south of Sandy. It is one of the few remaining examples of water-meadow in the valley of the River Ivel, and frequently floods in winter and spring. Despite the presence of that introduced horror, the American Mink, Water Voles can still sometimes be heard and seen, their presence revealed by the distinctive 'plop' as one enters the water from its bankside hole. Look also for the voles' larders (carefully collected and stacked shoots of tender grass) and their latrines, which may reveal their presence, even if you do not see or hear them. (TL165487)

These places – and also the other 93 local reserves – are treats in store if you are not already familiar with them. We owe their continued existence to the Wildlife Trusts, which acquired them, and now manages them in the ways necessary to maintain or improve their wildlife interest. You can find out more details by visiting www.wildlifebcnp.org/reserves

First published in *Bedfordshire County Life Magazine* in spring 2012

The infamous two-bird switch

Most naturalists are dedicated amateur or professional scientists, who record what they find in order to contribute to basic data sets for use in conservation and the study of population changes. Some birdwatchers and birders, however, are a different breed, with competition and list collection of primary importance to them. With this different attitude, rivalries may develop and, with them, suspicion and doubt concerning other observers' records. This comes to a head occasionally, when Observer A reports a rare bird and Observer B and his friends visit the site and find, not the bird that Observer A said that he saw, but a very similar species. Doubt? Nay, there is the near certainty (in their minds) that Observer A made a terrible mistake. Observer A, of course, insists that he was right, and that a different individual must have replaced his bird. A likely story!

I have come across this infamous 'two-bird switch' twice in my life. The first occasion was when I was still at school, in Kent, in 1954. Every day, on the way to school and again when returning home in the evening, I made counts of all the birds that I saw in the park that lay between my school and my home. On one May afternoon, I found a Caspian Tern fishing over the park lake. This was a very rare bird indeed, with only 30 previous British records ever. I took notes and then rushed to a telephone to alert a couple of fellow birdwatchers, including the Kent Ornithological Society's recorder. Some 40 minutes later, the three of us were watching a Common Tern fishing over the lake, and there was no sign whatsoever of a 'Caspian Tern'.

In those days, any tern was unusual inland, and this was,

indeed, the first record of a Common Tern at this particular lake. You can imagine how I felt. And exactly what my companions thought.

Luckily for me, the Caspian Tern reappeared the next day, being re-found by a fourth observer (who had not heard about my previous observation) and was watched for some time by him and later by one of my companions from the day before, the county bird recorder. Subsequently, an account of the occurrence was published in the journal *British Birds*.

If that Caspian Tern had moved on and had not stayed for two days, my reputation would have been destroyed, since nobody would have believed this two-bird switch.

The second occasion came 11 years later and involved a very famous ornithologist and multiple two-bird switches at Cape Clear Bird Observatory in Co. Cork. Professor M. F. M. (Maury) Meiklejohn, who was then one of the 'Ten Rare Men' (a member of the British Birds Rarities Committee that sits in judgment on all records of rare birds reported in Britain), was staying on the island. In the course of one month, there were five instances of the two-bird switch.

First, I found a Wood Lark (a very rare bird in Ireland) on a tiny area of burnt heather; but when the professor went to look for it, there was only a moulting Sky Lark, with a very short tail (one of the features of a Wood Lark), on the same burnt patch. It took three more visits to that burnt area before he saw the Wood Lark and I saw the Sky Lark.

Apart from Oystercatchers, Common Snipe and Curlews, all waders are rare on the island, so finding a Common Redshank on the only small lough was a highlight; but when the area was revisited the only wader at the lough was a Spotted Redshank, the first record for the island.

Then, the professor found a Green Sandpiper at one of the

island's three bogs, and the next day there was a Wood Sandpiper at the adjacent bog.

In a period rather short on migrant landbirds, a Pied Flycatcher on a dead twig in one of the gardens was one day's highlight, but observers who went to look for it found a Spotted Flycatcher on the very same twig.

Later that month, a Long-eared Owl was seen perched on a post. Yes, you've guessed it – the next bird to be seen perched on that post was a Short-eared Owl.

Of the ten birds involved in these five two-bird switches in September 1965, all but one (the Green Sandpiper) were eventually seen by all the observers involved, so there really were two birds in every case, not mere excuses for misidentifications. This extraordinary run of coincidences seems unlikely ever to be repeated, but the next time that some poor birder's claimed rarity is replaced by a commoner but similar bird, I hope that the doubters will remember that genuine two-bird switches *do* sometimes occur.

First published in *Bedfordshire County Life Magazine* in summer 2012

More highlights

Earlier, under the title 'Highlights', I described some of my most exciting wildlife encounters over the past 60 years. Here are a couple more.

One of the best trips that I ever made came as the result of an out-of-the-blue phone call from a friend. "I'm off to Kenya and Rwanda in a couple of weeks' time. Do you fancy joining me?" Well, of course I did. Quickly, I calculated that, by working two 84-hour weeks for the next fortnight, I could get sufficiently ahead in my schedule to take the time off, and my wife generously agreed to approve the expense and to take on all the parental responsibilities while I was away. Within the hour, therefore, I could phone back with an enthusiastic "Yes!"

The birds and mammals of Kenya were, of course, as thrilling as expected. African Elephants, Lions, Cheetahs, Giraffes, White Rhinoceroses, Black Rhinoceroses, Warthogs, Hippopotamuses and so on cannot fail to enthral, but are expected to do so. It would be a great disappointment not to see them and to revel in doing so. The greatest thrills come, however, from the unexpected encounters.

I am almost – but not quite – ashamed to admit the full circumstances of one of the two best encounters on this trip. We were staying at a select coastal hotel right on the beach a few miles from Mombassa and had a recreational day of rest after a series of daily dawn and dusk safaris had exhausted us. Staying at the same hotel were a bevy of models, their manager, director and photographer, engaged in a photo-shoot for an advertising calendar. "How," questioned my eager companion, "can we separate some of the girls from their manager?" I had no idea, but he did. He hired a launch along with its skipper and crew for a day, told the models that we were going out in search of whales and would any of them like to join us. Three would, and did, wearing teeny bikinis which, once we were a short distance offshore, very soon became monokinis. My friend's plan had worked beyond his wildest dreams, but this was not the highlight of the trip. After about half an hour of 'looking for whales' (which never appeared), we suddenly realised that a truly gigantic fish was accompanying the boat. It had a broad, square-ended head and its sleek grey body was covered with white spots. A Whale Shark! My friend and I immediately turned our attentions wholly to this wonderful beast – the World's largest fish, even bigger than a Basking Shark (the largest reaching a length of over 40 feet) – and a totally unexpected sighting. At one point, the shark, which was considerably longer than our launch, swam beneath the boat, with its head visible on one side and its tail on the other. Fantastic!

Our skipper would not allow us to swim with the shark, since, although the docile, plankton-eating Whale Shark is harmless, he knew that other less benign sharks were numerous in the same area. A little way back to shore, however, we and the girls snorkelled together over a coral reef. It was like swimming with mermaids. Why do I remember it all so clearly? It was 6th December. My birthday.

Despite being memorable, none of this was, however, the real highlight of our trip. That came in Rwanda. We were there just before the awful ethnic war between the Hutus and the Tutsis, so, away from the grossly overcrowded towns and villages, we were able just to enjoy the wildlife. Our main 'target' was, of course, the Mountain Gorillas, so before dawn one day we started the trek up the side of a heavily wooded extinct volcano. As the day got hotter, the slope got steeper, until we had to haul ourselves up one step at a time by holding onto the thick stems of the bamboos that dominated the vegetation. We were accompanied by a couple of armed guards-cum-guides, who searched for and then found the gorillas' overnight 'nest' of bamboo leaves. They also tracked the band of gorillas, from the disturbed plants and the group's droppings, and urged us on with "They are climbing faster than we are. If they reach the rim of the volcano before we do, we shall not be able to follow them...." With such encouragement, we climbed as fast as we could, sweat pouring from our bodies in the humidity of the enclosed jungle. We feared that we would never catch up with the gorillas, and it was clear that our guides thought so too. Then, suddenly, just in front of us, there they were. The gorillas had stopped for a rest. The oldest silverback male lay on his back chewing a bamboo shoot with a baby gorilla playing on his stomach. When the youngster became adventurous and climbed rather too high in a nearby bamboo, the silverback extended a long, hairy arm, cupped the baby in his huge hand and returned it to the safety of his belly. The females and young males were idly foraging or resting. They looked at us. We looked at them. Our eyes met. Theirs were dark brown and seemed to probe deeply into ours. What were they thinking? One female walked past me, brushing my arm with hers as she did so. This little group was obviously used to seeing human beings, and they showed no fear, indeed almost ignored us. With a diet composed almost wholly of vegetable material, this clearly has much the same effect on gorillas as would a diet of Brussels sprouts and baked beans on us. Their burps, belches and worse punctuated the silence. Taking care not to disturb or intrude upon this family scene, we sat, stood or squatted quietly, just a few yards away. We watched for half an hour, and then left them in peace. Wonderful! Magical! I'm a birdwatcher, but I can't remember a single bird from that morning. It belonged to the Mountain Gorillas. Gentle giants.

First published in *Bedfordshire County Life Magazine* in autumn 2012

Mountain Gorillas in Rwanda in December 1989 (*J. T. R. Sharrock*)

You never know

This year has been extraordinary, with a drought and hosepipe bans in late winter and spring, followed by the wettest summer for 100 years, and hot spells suddenly giving way to cold snaps. It was not good for most of our birds, with many broods of tits found dead in nest-boxes, probably starved rather than chilled, and Barn Owls in nest-boxes fared little better. Nestlings in natural nest-sites will doubtless have been similarly affected by the unpredictable and often unseasonable weather.

Despite this, there are always fascinating things for a naturalist to observe or discover. If you are interested in wildlife, life is never boring, and you never know what you will find next.

This summer, many lawns – including mine – were covered with the raised humps of ants' nests where in previous years there had been only one or two. Was it a particularly good year for ants? I don't think so. It seems much more likely that the ground was so waterlogged that the ants had to make their tunnels and chambers higher in the soil than usual. In a normal year, these nests would all have been much deeper and we would have been blissfully unaware of their presence. This may have been disruptive for the ants and annoying for those gardeners who like an immaculate lawn, but it was Heaven for the Green Woodpeckers that come to our gardens and its short-cropped grassland to feed on the ants.

The strange spring and summer, particularly the exceptionally wet weather, was probably responsible for the low number of butterflies. By early autumn, the purple flowers of *Buddleia* (colloquially known as 'the Butterfly Bush') should have been covered in butterflies feeding on the nectar, but often were not. It's a non-random unscientific survey, but I always count every butterfly that I see, and in the summer of 2012 my total was only 60% of my average for the previous four years. Hardest hit was the Small Tortoiseshell, and during the whole of 2012 I saw only nine individuals of this beautiful species, which is often thought of as one of our commonest butterflies. In this case, however, the weather may not be the whole story, for there is some evidence that a parasitic fly (*Sturmia bella*) attacks Small Tortoiseshell caterpillars more often than it does those of other related butterflies.

It was while looking for one of our rarest butterflies, the tiny Duke of Burgundy, that I was intrigued to see small, black-and-red bees frantically zigzagging low over short chalk-hillside turf, apparently searching for something. This behaviour was new to me, as was the bee species, so I investigated further. To my surprise, they were looking for empty snail shells, and I subsequently learnt that this species of bee (*Osmia bicolor*) actually builds its nest inside these shells.

Although often regarded as a weed by gardeners, Ivy is a wonderful plant for wildlife, and − in my view − should be a feature of every garden. It provides nest-sites for Wrens, Dunnocks, Robins and thrushes in spring and summer, and its berries are food for birds and small mammals in early winter, but its greatest value is the nectar in its flowers, which appear in late summer and early autumn, when most other flowers have gone. It was while admiring immaculate, newly emerged Red Admiral butterflies feeding on Ivy flowers that I spotted a giant among the many hoverflies that were also nectaring.

Many species of hoverfly resemble bees, and this imitation doubtless ensures that they are preyed upon less often by birds that are fooled just as we are by the deceptive appearance. The giant hoverfly, however, was not only bigger than all the others, but its thorax was chestnut-coloured and its head and abdomen were black-and-yellow. It so closely resembled a Hornet that I had at first mistaken it for one. Eventually, I was able to photograph it and its identity as the Hornet-mimic Hoverfly (*Volucella zonaria*) was confirmed for me by hoverfly expert John O'Sullivan. Reading about this species, I learnt that there were only two records for the United Kingdom prior to 1940, and this superb insect is still largely confined to southern England, but has been spreading northwards in recent years. Its mimicry of a Hornet not only protects it from predation, but is also an essential element of its life history. The adults enter Hornet nests and are not attacked by the Hornets, lay their eggs inside the nest and the hoverfly larvae then feed on the Hornet larvae, pupate in the nest and emerge as adult hoverflies unscathed. Thus, it fools not only predators and us, but also the very creatures that it mimics.

Thus, casual observations of animals and plants can often lead to very surprising discoveries. This time, I shall end with a question, to be answered in the next article. What animal, which I am certain you will find in your garden, carries its young in a marsupium, just like a kangaroo?

First published in *Bedfordshire County Life Magazine* in winter 2012/13

What's in a name?

After the year 2012, with its wildly changeable weather, we must surely all be hoping that 2013 is a bit more 'normal'? A frosty start, some April showers, a balmy summer, a glowing autumn, then it's winter again. We – and the wildlife – can cope with that. This spring and summer, we'll discover what effects last year's excesses have had upon the delicate interactions between the plants and animals in the countryside and in our gardens.

Observing wildlife does not necessarily demand expeditions to remote places abroad, or even remote parts of our county. Our own garden or a nearby public park can be the location for an interesting or even exciting encounter. At the end of the last article (on page 142), I posed the question: What animal, which I am certain you will find in your garden, has a marsupium, just like a kangaroo? The answer is the woodlouse, of which there are about 45 species found in the United Kingdom. The female carries her two or three dozen eggs in a pouch on her underside. Turn over any log, decaying plant remains and most rocks almost anywhere and these 'little armadillos' trot away on their 14 legs or roll up into balls like scaly hedgehogs (these ones will be in the aptly named genus *Armadillidium*). They are so familiar to us, yet live fascinating lives to which we have probably never given a thought. They are not insects, but are the only crustaceans that do not live in water. Unlike crabs and lobsters, they are not edible, having an unpleasant taste (so I am informed). Perhaps reflecting the fact that they are intriguingly unusual in appearance, woodlice have a large number of local names, including pill-bug, roly-poly and chuggy-pig.

My own garden provided me with two discoveries last year. The first of these was the Hornet-mimic Hoverfly (*Volucella zonaria*) feeding on Ivy flowers, which I described in the previous article. I came across the second when engaged in one of my least-favourite jobs, weeding a flowerbed. There, for the first time in 38 years, I found not one but scores of plants of the delightfully named and pretty little herb, Enchanter's-nightshade (*Circaea lutetiana*). By referring to the local botanical atlas, I found that this was the first time that this common woodland plant had been recorded in the tetrad (2-km x 2-km square) in which I live. Its English and scientific names reflect the fact that it is supposed to have been used in her magic by the enchantress Circe of Greek mythology. The plant spreads vegetatively by means of rhizomes and its seeds as small burrs in the wool or hair of mammals (or on our clothing), and I was warned by fellow gardeners that it could soon become an invasive weed throughout my garden. I do not mind if it does. A weed is a plant where it is not wanted, and I *want* to have this plant, with its attractive small white flowers, in my garden.

The same bed also held another of my favourite wild flowers, the Scarlet Pimpernel. The association with the hero of Baroness Orczy's novels may add glamour to this plant, but it has a long flowering period, so its bright-red, five-petalled flowers were still on show during my late-October weeding. The flowers react quickly to light changes, closing before dusk or in overcast conditions, as soon as a cloud obscures the sun. This has given rise to several country names for the plant, such as Shepherd's Weatherglass and Poor-man's Barometer. It was regarded as a magical plant, providing protection from evil spirits, and cures for a wide variety of illnesses were attributed to it, based on the legend that its flowers were formed by drops falling from Christ on the cross. Although poisonous in large doses, extract of Scarlet Pimpernel is still used even today in some herbal remedies for rheumatism, liver and kidney diseases. The seed capsule resembles a pepper-pot, which is probably the origin of the second part of the English name, Pimpernel.

On warm days in spring and summer, you may see a 'bee' shaped rather like a V-bomber, with swept-back wings and a long, pointed 'nose', zipping around, suddenly stopping and then remaining absolutely stationary in flight, and then zipping away again or even flying backwards. Brown and 'furry', it looks just like a peculiar bee, but it is actually a fly, one of the many species of bee-fly. The most common and first to appear in spring is the Greater Bee-fly (*Bombylius major*). Its resemblance to a bee may protect it from predators, although it is harmless and has no sting or bite. The vicious-looking long 'nose' is a rigid proboscis (often three or four times the length of the head), which is modified for feeding on nectar and pollen within tube-like flowers. The bee-fly's larvae are parasitic in the nests of solitary bees, wasps or beetles, and the adult bee-fly often lays her eggs near the entrance hole of the host's nest or burrow. These eggs may be laid in flight, the female (looking like a bomber) dropping them like little bombs. She has also been observed subsequently dust-bathing and then flying back to distribute this dust over the top of the eggs by shaking it from her 'fur'. The eggs may also be laid on flowers where bees may visit and take the eggs accidentally back to their nests. In our area, April is often the best month in which to see these splendid little animals.

First published in *Bedfordshire County Life Magazine* in spring 2013

What's in a garden?

Over the years, I have come across quite a collection of interesting wildlife 'things' in my garden, and most people with an established plot will (or could) have done the same.

Perhaps the most surprising discovery came when I was using a broom to push up the branches of a large Lilac bush heavy with flowers. "Boing!", something landed on my bald head, bounced off and lay unconscious on the ground, having knocked itself out. Small and furry, it was obviously a mouse or a vole, but I was astonished when I picked it up to find that it was a Harvest Mouse: tiny, rather vole-like, with a blunt nose, rounded ears and a long tail. I carried it indoors and put it in a large jar, so that I could watch it when it recovered, which it soon did. Surprisingly, it did not seem frightened when I put my hand in the jar, and it happily sat on my hand and wrapped its tail around one of my fingers, for this – our smallest rodent – has a prehensile tail, which helps it to climb around in the vegetation which it prefers as its natural habitat. That does not normally include Lilac trees.

I am rather unusual among birdwatchers in that I do not keep a list of all the species that I have seen in the United Kingdom or in the World and do not go twitching to see a bird that other people have found, even if it would be a 'new' species for me. I do, however, keep a list of the birds that nest in my garden. Over the years, some have gone and others have come. When I first moved to my present home, 36 years ago, Lesser Redpolls and Tree Sparrows nested in the garden, but are now long-gone. House Sparrows and Starlings used to nest in the roof, but do so no longer. Willow Warblers, with their wonderful descending, tinkling trill, nested every year, but have now been replaced by their look-alike, the Chiffchaff, with its monotonous, repetitive, two-note song. The most recent loss is Spotted Flycatcher, sadly no longer occupying the nest-box just a couple of metres from my study window. The most recent gain - but perhaps a one-off, was a pair of Mallards that nested beside my tiny garden pond, the female wonderfully camouflaged among the vegetation of a little bog-garden.

Exciting migrants and casual visitors over the years have included singing Wood Warblers (twice), a Firecrest, a Little Egret, pairs of Mandarin Ducks, a Raven and a remarkable string of raptors, including Merlin, Osprey and Goshawk, in addition to the expected Kestrel, Sparrowhawk, Common Buzzard and Hobby. I am, however, still awaiting my first Red Kite in or over the garden. I have also never had a migrant Common Redstart or Pied Flycatcher in the garden, surprising omissions after 36 years of garden-birdwatching.

A total of 22 species of butterfly includes nothing exciting, though Walls were regular in the early years, but then vanished until just one recent sighting. Interesting large moths have included Lime, Eyed, Poplar, Privet and Hummingbird Hawk-moths, an Old Lady and regular Red Underwings, while the most interesting larva was the extraordinary black-and-yellow striped caterpillar of the Alder Moth, which has long, club-ended, black hairs. I had always wanted to find one of these, having seen an illustration in a book when I was a schoolboy, so it was a red-letter day when I spotted one inching its way down the trunk of a Hawthorn tree prior to pupating.

Interesting plants turn up now and then. In one year, my lawn was dotted with hundreds of the beautiful, multicoloured Wild Pansy or Heartsease *Viola tricolor*; the next year there was none (and I do not use herbicides). Indeed, a lawn can be fascinating if you leave it alone and do not demand that it consist of nothing but boring green grass. Mine is as much moss as grass, and delightfully soft underfoot as a result. Currently, it contains many deep-purple Sweet Violets *Viola odorata*. 'Weeds' in flower borders have included the delicate Enchanter's-nightshade *Circaea lutetiana* more typical of woodland and the strange Wild Arum (also known as Cuckoo-pint and Lords-and-Ladies) *Arum maculatum* which attracts and traps flies, later releasing them to carry out pollination. These plants are not unwanted by me, so are not 'weeds' in my garden.

Plants often have so many vernacular English names (some of which are applied to more than one species) that it is necessary to use their scientific names (often erroneously called 'Latin names').

The mossy lawn often has fungi of various sorts, including puffballs, spurting smoke-like plumes of spores when accidentally run over by the mower. This year, I found a concentration of the even-more-strange-looking earthstars under a Holly bush, identified by fungus expert Alan Outen as *Geastrum fimbriatum*, one of the half-dozen similar species found in our area. How can one not be intrigued by such an odd-looking object?

Mine is a mature garden, tended for the benefit of wildlife – so I claim, though other people might describe it as 'overgrown, untidy and uncared-for' – but every garden will have lots of wildlife interest if only someone looks for it.

First published in *Bedfordshire County Life Magazine* in summer 2013

Twitching

I have stated before that I am a birdwatcher (or birder, in today's parlance), but not a twitcher. There are, however, times when twitching is the only recourse.

Although unlikely, a Wallcreeper or a Snowy Owl might one day turn up in our inland county, but one could wait a lifetime and never see a Hazel Grouse – there is just no chance that this non-migratory, sedentary species would arrive here naturally. The same is true of many mammals, reptiles, amphibians and even flying insects, such as some moths and butterflies. I have seen Monarch butterflies several times in Ireland, which certainly crossed either the Atlantic from North America or at least vast distances over the sea from the Canary Islands, and they could conceivably penetrate as far inland as our area. Painted Lady butterflies get here from North Africa every year (and who can forget the invasion of millions in May 2009?), and we could live in hope of seeing a migrant Queen of Spain Fritillary (which even colonised coastal Suffolk briefly in recent years). A Grey Seal has travelled up the River Great Ouse and thereby added its name to the lists of mammals seen not only in Cambridgeshire, but also in Bedfordshire. The Glanville Fritillary, however, is a butterfly long-gone from our area (though perhaps occurred in the seventeenth century, when it was still present in Lincolnshire), and is now confined in the UK to the southern cliffs of the Isle of Wight and a few sites in nearby Hampshire. There, it is wholly sedentary.

Now, perhaps, it is clear why three of us travelled to the Isle of Wight this summer, to see Glanville Fritillary. Needing warm, dry, sunny, windless days, when these butterflies were flying, our three days there were plagued by the cool, cloudy, windy conditions prevailing in early summer 2013. We failed to see a Glanville Fritillary, but we did have some successes.

I can remember when it was possible to see wild, native Red Squirrels in Norfolk, and I have seen them in Scotland and Ireland, but they have been ousted by the introduced North American Tree Rat (also known more politely as the Grey Squirrel) from almost the whole of England and Wales. The Reds do survive, however, on the Isle of Wight and on Brownsea Island in Poole Harbour, where the Grey has not penetrated. Even on a dull, drizzly day, we had wonderful views of the magnificent Red Squirrel, with its bronzed red coat, golden-tipped, bushy tail and tufted ears, just as Beatrix Potter's Squirrel Nutkin or Little Grey Rabbit's companion in Alison Uttley's books should look. This had been our secondary target on our trip to the Isle of Wight.

Our third success, however, was a surprise. We did not know that the southern European Wall Lizard had been introduced to the Isle of Wight and that there was a thriving population around Ventnor, where we stayed for three days. In the Botanic Garden there, we had marvellous, close views of a male and a female sunning themselves on a rock in the evening on one of those rare occasions when the sun did appear. Larger than our native Common Lizard, these were gorgeous beasts, beautifully patterned in black, red, yellow, orange, white and green.

Thus, we can justify our twitching expedition, since we would never see a wild Red Squirrel or a non-captive Wall Lizard in our part of England, however long we waited. The Glanville Fritillary will have to wait until next year ...

First published in *Bedfordshire County Life Magazine* in autumn 2013

Watch out!

The patterns and shapes of animals have evolved for a variety of reasons, perhaps because they create an advantage over competitors, or they help to foil enemies or they assist congeners.

The first time that I saw a Tiger in the wild was in Khao Yai National Park in Thailand. It emerged from the long Elephant Grass and strolled across an open area where deer were grazing. The deer paid almost no attention to it, presumably being aware from its attitude and gait that it was not in hunting mode. What especially drew my attention, however, were the large, gleaming white patches on the rear of the Tiger's ears. I had never noticed these patches before, on captive Tigers in zoos, probably because the Tigers were usually looking at me and I was not seeing a rear view. Why should Tigers have such an obvious feature? I can only imagine that it is a signal to other Tigers following behind, so is a way that cubs keep in contact with their mother.

In a way, this equates to the Rabbit's white tail, which flashes when it runs away from a predator, serving as a warning to other Rabbits. The white tails or white patches on the rear of many species of deer serve the same purpose.

A less-well-known feature is the patches on the back of the head of many species of raptor. As described back in winter 2001 (pages 6-7), I first noticed this when I was leaning on a gate at dusk at Gibraltar Point in Lincolnshire and a female Sparrowhawk flew in and perched a dozen or so metres in front of me. It clearly had not noticed me, since it perched with its back to me, and there – 'staring at me' – was a pair of 'eyes', two pale patches on the back of the

Sparrowhawk's head. If I had been a larger predator, I might have been deterred from attaching that otherwise vulnerable prey, since superficially it certainly looked as if it was aware of my presence. Since then, I have noticed that many other birds of prey (including owls) similarly have 'eyes in the back of their heads'. This must convey an advantage of some sort and predator deterrence seems the most obvious.

Quite a number of butterflies and moths also have 'false eyes,' but these must serve a different purpose, presumably diverting a predator's attack from the actual head and body (better to lose a bit of wing than be killed). The familiar Peacock butterfly is an obvious example, but there are many others, including moths such as the Emperor, which, like the Peacock, has 'eyes' on both its forewings and its hindwings.

It is well known, of course, that some lizards take this sacrifice of part of the body in the event of an attack to the extreme, shedding their tail (which continues to writhe) while they make their escape. They then have the ability to grow a new tail.

All these features will have conveyed an advantage, thereby leading to the possessors being more likely to survive and procreate, passing on the advantage to future generations. The effectiveness is apparent even to us when we try to find the nest of, say, a brooding female Mallard or Pheasant and can barely detect her amongst vegetation even from just a metre or so away, so effective is her camouflage. That, of course, is why many female birds are dull and brown whereas the males are brightly coloured. When the parental roles are reversed – as with phalaropes (small wading birds), the males of which incubate the eggs – it is the male that is the duller of the two sexes.

These musings were sparked by two separate observations

– of the Tiger and the Sparrowhawk – many years ago. Much more recently, we have probably all been aware that this autumn that has just passed was exceptionally good for fungi. Presumably, the combination of occasional rain and warm days created just the right conditions for many species to produce fruiting bodies. In my own village, the local churchyard suddenly sprouted a larger horde of mushrooms than I have ever seen before. I could not resist counting them and the total was a staggering 655. They looked delicious, they smelled delicious, but, unfortunately, fungus expert Alan Outen identified them as the Yellow-staining Mushroom. This can be eaten with no ill effects by some people, but others may suffer vomiting and diarrhoea for several days, and eating them can even lead to coma in extreme cases. Be warned! Although they look exceedingly similar, it is easy to distinguish them from the edible Field Mushroom by slicing the base of the stipe (the stem) with a knife, when that of the poisonous Yellow-staining Mushroom turns bright yellow.

The warm, sunny days of late autumn also brought forth butterflies that in some years would already have been hibernating or have succumbed to the cold. Brimstones, Commas, Peacocks, Small Tortoiseshells, Speckled Woods and Red Admirals were still flying in my garden after the *Buddleia* flowers had nearly all gone to seed. The first four species all overwinter in England as hibernating adults, hidden away amongst ivy or in our garages and garden sheds. The Speckled Wood, which has increasingly become familiar in our gardens as it has spread in recent years, is unique among British butterflies in that it overwinters both as a caterpillar and as a pupa, resulting in several overlapping generations in the following summer. Of the six butterflies mentioned, only the Red Admiral seldom survives a wet, cold

English winter. Debatably the most beautiful of all our butterflies, the Red Admiral is an immigrant, and, like the Painted Lady, those that we see in spring and summer have all crossed the English Channel and perhaps also the Mediterranean to reach us from the Continent or North Africa.

First published in *Bedfordshire County Life Magazine* in winter 2013/14

Answers to Wildlife Puzzles

1. The valuable molluscan product is a PEARL, produced by an oyster; the North American name for the Common Seal is HARBOR Seal; and it was on 7th December 1941, described at the time by US President Franklin Delano Roosevelt as "a date which will live in infamy," that the Japanese attacked the American naval base at PEARL HARBOR in Hawaii.

2. JINX. The Wryneck was formerly called the Jynx (and its modern scientific name is *Jynx torquilla*). It is a bark-coloured, camouflaged, migratory woodpecker that now seldom nests in Britain, although it was widespread in the 19th century and even into the middle of the 20th century. In recent years, an average of about one per year has been seen in Bedfordshire. Its modern English name of Wryneck (and also another old name for it of Snake-bird) refer to its ability to turn its head through more than 360°. In the past, it was caught and tied to a wheel for the casting of spells that involved 'turning' or 'returning' events, hence 'putting a jinx on' someone or something.

3. WHIPSNADE (where there is a white LION cut in the chalk hillside). The other links are with *The LION, the Witch and the Wardrobe* by C. S. Lewis, the LIONFISH that frequents the coral-reefs of the Red Sea and Indian Ocean and which has spines which inject venom; and the seed-head of the Dandelion, which is also known as a DANDELION CLOCK.

4. RAINBOW TROUT. The seven colours of the rainbow are derived in sequence from: (1) RED Admiral, (2) ORANGE-tip, (3) YELLOWhammer, (4) GREEN Woodpecker (Professor Yaffle), (5) BLUEbell, (6) INDIGO Bunting, and (7) VIOLET (from A. A. Milne's Winnie the Pooh stories)

5. TIMBER. The lines between Broom and Oakley and between Greenfield and Hatch cross at Wood Farm (north of Old Warden and west of Ickwell).

6. THE GRAND SURPRISE (an old name for the Camberwell Beauty butterfly). The other names pair up as follows: 2d, 3e, 4b, 5f, 6h, 7g, 8a and 9e.

7. KING DAVID II OF SCOTLAND (1324-1371) was the son of Robert the Bruce. Père DAVID's Deer, named after Père (later Abbe) Armand David, was saved from extinction in China when the world's largest

155

captive herd was established in Woburn Park. Often whispering so as not to disturb the wildlife, Sir DAVID Attenborough's romp with Gorillas was one highlight in his long television career. The ascetic St DAVID, patron saint of Wales, died on 1st March in about AD 589.

8. The shopkeeper cleans up (Butcher's-broom), the stockman protects his money (Shepherd's-purse) and the cleric has no need for a hat (Monk's-hood)

9. MONARCH, the pinnacle of the British ruling classes. They are all butterflies (Grizzled Skipper, Comma, Gatekeeper, Ringlet and Monarch), of which the Monarch is the rarest. The answers were all straightforward, except, perhaps, the quote:

"She had a dark and a roving eye, And her hair hung down in ringlets; She was a nice girl, a proper girl, But one of the roving kind"

which comes from the 1951 song *The Roving Kind* by Guy Mitchell, based on an 1800s traditional English folksong, *The Pirate Ship*.

10. What's left after a fire is ASH, the complete name of a tree. (The other trees, which were unfinished, were MAPle, CHESTnut, WILLow, POPlar, BEEch and HORNbeam.)

11. SUMMER (the plants are Springbeauty, Autumn Lady's-tresses and Common Wintergreen)

12. SWEET VIOLET and GALLANT SOLDIER. All of them, except Sweet Violet, are non-native and occur in Britain only as escapes from cultivation. All of them are European species, except Gallant Soldier, which originated in South America.

13. REDSHANK (which is the name of a bird and a plant, whereas the others are all the names of moths and also the name of either a bird or a plant)

14. The English names Londonpride and London-rocket both include the name of the capital city, whereas the names Dartford Warbler, Brent Goose, Camberwell Beauty and Deptford Pink each include merely the name of a nearby town or borough of London.

15. Otter *Lutra lutra*, Merlin *Falco columbarius*, Elk *Alces alces*, Daisy *Bellis perennis*, Fulmar *Fulmarus glacialis*, Hop *Humulus lupulus* and Box *Buxus sempervirens*.

16. The link is CIRCUS. The three species of raptor known as harriers that breed in Britain are Montagu's (named after Lt-Col. George Montagu), Hen (domesticated chickens are descended from the Asian Red Jungle-fowl), and Marsh. The scientific generic name of all three harriers is *CIRCUS* (*Circus pygargus*, *Circus cyaneus* and *Circus aeruginosus*).

17. MAJOR (the fish is the Sergeant Major and the scientific names of the Great Spotted Woodpecker, the Great Tit and the Curly Waterweed are *Dendrocopos major, Parus major* and *Lagarosiphon major*).

18. They are or were all symbols of wildlife organisations in Bedfordshire. (The Avocet represented the Royal Society for the Protection of Birds, which has its national headquarters at The Lodge in Sandy; the Badger is the emblem of The Wildlife Trusts, the Bedfordshire branch of which is based at Priory Park in Bedford; the Hobby is featured on the logo of the Bedfordshire Bird Club, and *The Hobby* is the title of its newsletter; while the Muntjac is the symbol of the Bedfordshire Natural History Society.)

19. BANEBERRY (with a man's name in its alternative name of Herb Christopher, whereas the others all have a lady's name in their alternative names: Cob-nut is Hazel, Gladdon is Stinking Iris, King-cup is Marsh Marigold and Ling is Heather; Baneberry is also the only one of the five which is the plant's official English name)

20. Pasque Flower, Crocodile, Fieldfare, Grey Squirrel and Scarce Chaser

21. UPCHER'S WARBLER is the odd one out (Common Shelduck, Manx Shearwater, Crab-plover, Northern Wheatear, Atlantic Puffin and Common Kingfisher all habitually nest in underground holes)

22. (1) Newt. (2) Rook. (3) Wasp. (4) Broom

23. They are all components of the Solar System: (1) SUNdew, (2) MOONwort, (3) EARTHnut, (4) VENUS's-looking-glass, and (5) Dog's-MERCURY

24. IN A PALACE   (King Penguin; Lords-and-Ladies; Duke of Burgundy; footman; Monarch; and Queen of Spain Fritillary), with the footman being the lowliest

25. STOAT (Beavers live in a Lodge, Foxes in an Earth, a Hare in a Form, Otters in a Holt, Rabbits in a Burrow and Squirrels in a Drey)

26. JACK (Jack Snipe, Jack-go-to-bed-at-noon and Jackdaw)

27. Beelzebub, the Devil, Lucifer or Satan (Devil-bird, Devil-screamer, Devil-screecher and so on are all old country names for the Swift; the Small Manta is also known as the Devil-ray; Orange Hawkweed is also called Devil's Paintbrush; the scientific name of the Widemouth Blindcat is *Satan eurystomus*, and Marsh Fritillary caterpillars feed on Devil's-bit Scabious)

28. At the card table, (a) *ACEr*, (c) KING crab, (d) QUEEN of Spain Fritillary, and (b) JACKdaw

29. 1 Large Copper. 2 Banded Demoiselle. 3 Yellow Wagtail. 4 Fat-hen. 5 Cinnabar. 6 Badger.

30. Vertebrate body organs (the plants are LUNGwort, KIDNEY Vetch and SPLEENwort)

31. Berry Drop Goose Leopard (can each be preceded by Snow)

Garden Ruby Scarlet Wood (are all Tiger moths)

Jersey Pale Purple Sand (are all Toadflaxes)

Ruff Sorrel Vetch Warbler (can each be preceded by Wood)

32. TEAL (the others all make up rhyming pairs)

33. PRUNELLA: the plant and the bird both have the generic scientific name of *Prunella* (*Prunella vulgaris* and *Prunella modularis*) and Sybil Fawlty was played by the actress Prunella Scales

34. Bearded Tit, Bee Moth, Bristly Goat's-beard, Goat Willow, Moustached Warbler, Scarlet Tiger, Spectacled Bear, Whiskered Bat

35. They each feature in the title of a book, a film or a play (the James Bond film *Goldeneye* written by Michael France, the book *The Snow Goose* by Paul Gallico, the children's book *Great Northern* by Arthur Ransome, the play *The Sociable Plover* by Tim Whitnall, and the film *Tawny Pipit* starring Bernard Miles).

36. THEY ARE ALL BLACK.

37. They all have connections with the element SULPHUR (the butterfly is the Brimstone, the plant is Sulphur Clover, the fungus is Sulphur-tuft and the moth is the Cinnabar, which is the name given to a sulphide of mercury).

38. ONE is missing. (The others are TWO-tailed Pasha butterfly, a THREE-toed sloth, FOUR-spotted Chaser dragonfly, FIVE-bearded Rockling fish, SIX-spot Burnet moth, SEVEN Whistler is an old name for the Whimbrel, Figure of EIGHT moth, NINE-spotted moth, and TEN-spined Stickleback fish)

39. Each is the common name of two very different organisms (Butterbur is the plant *Petasites hybridus* and the moth *Hydraecia petasitis*; Common Swift is the bird *Apus apus* and the moth *Hepialus lupulinus*; Magpie is the bird *Pica pica* and the moth *Abraxas grossulariata*; Redshank is the bird *Tringa totanus* and the plant *Polygonum perspicaria*; Sycamore is the tree *Acer pseudoplatanus* and the moth *Acronicta aceris*; and Wormwood is the plant *Artemisia absinthium* and the moth *Cucullia absinthii*)

40. HOLLY (the only one where the vernacular name but not the scientific generic name, *Ilex*, is a girl's name; the reverse is the case with all the others: *Melissa, Erica, Veronica, Daphne, Prunella* and *Rosa*)

41. Brambling, Goldfinch, House Martin and Northern Wheatear (all have white rumps); Dipper, Long-tailed Tit, Penduline Tit and Wren (all build domed nests); Lapwing, Hoopoe, Shag and Waxwing (all have crests); Common Pheasant, Little Owl, Mandarin Duck and Red-legged Partridge (are all introduced, non-native species in the UK); Goldeneye, Great Tit, Nuthatch and Smew (all nest in holes)

42. BOG-MYRTLE (its alternative name is Sweet Gale, whereas the other two are also known as Stinkweed and Stinking Iris)

43. TONGUE (Adder's-tongue *Ophioglossum*, Hart's-tongue *Phyllitis* and Hound's-tongue *Cynoglossum* are all wild plants found in our area)

44. They all prey primarily on related animals (the Daddy-longlegs Spider feeds mainly on other spiders, the King Cobra feeds mainly on other snakes and the Sparrowhawk feeds mainly on other birds)

45. STOAT (all the others also have a meaning other than the name of a mammal or a bird)

46. Black Bryony, Avocet, Roseate Tern, Snipe, Great Crested Grebe, Song Thrush & Woodlark.

47. *Viola tricolor*, also called Wild Pansy or Heartsease.

48. SAP (from Spruce, Ash and Plane)

49. Two answers are equally correct. (1) Camberwell Beauty (the title of a play by Chris Ward, but never made into a film, whereas the others were: *Clouded Yellow* starring Trevor Howard & Jean Simmons in 1951, *Painted Lady* starring Helen Mirren in 1997 and *Peacock* starring Cillian Murphy in 2010) or (2) Clouded Yellow (which is in the family Pieridae, whereas the other three are all in the Nymphalidae)

50. LARK HILL, on the A6, between Wilstead and Clophill. (Bee, butterfly, fly, frog, lizard, monkey and spider [but not lark] are all names of British orchids. Desert, garden, marsh, reed, river, sedge, willow and wood [but not hill] are all names of British warblers.)

51. SANDPIPER (The chain is Garlic Penny-cress to Field Garlic to Field Vole to Water Vole to Water Dock to Wood Dock to Wood White)

52. SULPHUR TUFT (the numbers refer to the atomic numbers of the elements copper, silver, gold and sulphur, so the animals and plants referred to are Small Copper and Large Copper butterflies, Silver Birch, Goldfinch, the Sulphur Tuft fungus that appears commonly on rotting stumps and the moth Spotted Sulphur that has not been known in East Anglia since the 1960s)

Acknowledgments

The Editor of the quarterly *Bedfordshire County Life Magazine* kindly gave permission for these reminiscences and comments to be reprinted in book form. In a few places, the text has been amended to bring it up to date, to insert relevant additional information or to correct minor errors.

My regular Bridge partner, Bernard O'Connor, helped enormously with computational intricacies beyond my capabilities, and my first wife, Erika Sharrock, proofread the entire text.

I am grateful to my regular companions in the field, David Fisher and Alan Outen, who allowed the reproduction of their photographs on the front cover.

Cover photographs: Red Squirrel *Sciurus vulgaris* (and the author *Homo sapiens*) on the Isle of Wight, June 2013 (*David Fisher*); Fly Agarics *Amanita muscaria*, in the New Forest, Hampshire, September 1995 (*Alan Outen*)